Religious Education in
the Secondary School

The Roehampton Teaching Studies Series

This new series of books is aimed primarily at student and practising teachers. It covers key issues in current educational debate relating to age phases, school management, the curriculum and teaching methods. Each volume examines the topic critically, bringing out the practical implications for teachers and school organisation.

Authors - not necessarily based at Roehampton - are commissioned by an Editorial Board at The Roehampton Institute, one of the United Kingdom's leading centres of educational research as well as undergraduate and postgraduate training.

The General Editor of the series is Dr Jim Docking, formerly Chairman of the Institute's School of Education.

A selection of recent and forthcoming titles appears on the back cover of this book.

Religious Education in the Secondary School: Prospects for Religious Literacy

Andrew Wright

David Fulton Publishers

London
Published in association with the Roehampton Institute

David Fulton Publishers Ltd
2 Barbon Close, London WC1N 3JX

First published in Great Britain by
David Fulton Publishers 1993

British Library Cataloguing in Publication Data

A catalogue record for this book is available from the British Library

ISBN 1-85346-242-X

Typeset by RP Typesetters Ltd., Unit 13, 21 Wren Street, London WC1X 0HF.
Printed in Great Britain by BPCC Journals Ltd., Exeter.

Contents

Acknowledgements and Dedication

I owe an enormous debt to all those who, through the years, have taught me, all those whom I have taught alongside, and all those whom I have had the privilege of teaching. It is of course an almost impossible task to select out any by name, but I shall nevertheless take the risk. My sincere thanks go to, amongst many others, Andy Angel, Kathy Ashton, Jo Backus, Joy Barrow, Jonathan Galloway, Kristoph Koslowski, Salim Savani and the late Father Jim Lowry.

Jim Docking showed himself to be the wisest of editors, willing to give me the space to make my mistakes on my own before pointing out where I had gone wrong.

My own pilgrimage towards a deeper understanding of religion began, in the company of Jonathan, Heather and Angela, surrounded by the love and wisdom of my parents, Ruth and Bill. They nurtured not just their own children, but countless others who passed through a home whose door was always open.

Above all my gratitude and thanks must go to my wife Jacqueline and our two children Rebecca and Elizabeth. Their patience, understanding, love and humour have given me more than anyone could possibly deserve, and it is to them that this book is dedicated.

Andrew Wright
Whitelands College
Easter 1993

Introduction

Setting the scene

There is an old Chinese proverb that reads: 'Give someone a fish you feed them for a day. Teach them to fish, you feed them for life'. It is a proverb that has much to teach those of us concerned with religious education in secondary schools in a pluralistic western democracy in the late twentieth century. It can, I believe, illuminate our task of enabling pupils to become more intelligent, knowledgeable and perceptive about the way religious beliefs and religious questions help shape our understanding of ourselves, our society, our environment and the universe we inhabit.

This book is written specifically for those considering embarking on careers as teachers of religious education in secondary schools; those training for the profession on college and university PGCE courses; those currently facing the challenge of a first teaching post; and for those returning to the profession after a period of absence.

I hope it will be of some value to many others: teachers and heads of departments seeking a little refreshment and possibly a new vision; headteachers and governors; parents and guardians; those concerned with teacher training and the academic study of religious education; indeed anyone concerned with the development of individuals and society towards a wiser and deeper understanding of the profound questions which religion raises, and the complex and often contradictory answers humanity has given to these questions.

The challenge of the 1988 Education Reform Act

Religious education today is in a state of flux. The 1988 Education Reform Act marked one of the profoundest changes that education in general, and religious education in particular, has gone through in England and Wales this century. Indeed the only comparable development was that introduced by the revolutionary 1944 Education Act. The dust has yet to settle on the educational world, and only now are we beginning to see through the haze and get a feel for the implications of the changes the Act has brought about for teachers of religious education in schools and in classrooms.

One thing though does seem clear: the flourishing debate surrounding religious education following the implementation of the new legislation indicates that the Act does not offer a pre-packaged blueprint for the future shape of the subject. It offers a clear framework, but the way in which this framework is to be utilized in classrooms remains open to interpretation. We have the skeleton, but the flesh still needs to be added. We stand at a crossroads, uncertain as to which path to go down. Such uncertainty can breed anxiety and a hankering after the security of the past. Consequently there is a danger that, with religious education once again in the melting pot, we will fail to grasp the opportunity for growth, development and new vision.

To stay still for too long, to remain static and fixed in the traditional way of doing things, can be dangerous: we become complacent and the grass begins to grow beneath our feet. As teachers we pull the same old worksheets out of the filing cabinet year after year, we get stuck in the old routine, we start to stagnate, and the vigour and enthusiasm we used to bring to the subject begins to wane.

To move forward, to look for new vision and new paths, opens up the opportunity for growth. To experiment a little, to take the risk of trying out something different in the classroom, can be dangerous if things fail to work out as we had hoped. Yet this process of change, this willingness to have the courage to embrace the original, can open our work in classrooms to new potential, new possibilities.

Observing much of the debate surrounding the new situation faced by religious education with the advent of the 1988 Act has been a bit like watching a fly trapped in a bottle: buzzing frantically around, hitting its head against the sides in a desperate attempt to find a way forward, yet unable to see the rim and escape to a new future. Captivated by familiar models, past conversations and old agendas, the debate seeks to find ways of accommodating the old order into the new framework: old wine in new skins.

Given this situation, this book sets out to achieve two things. First, it aims to give a picture of the current state of play in religious education, to offer a clear introduction to the new legislation, and the problems and possibilities it lays before us. Only by understanding more clearly where exactly we are will we be able to move forward. Second, this book seeks to suggest ways in which the subject might develop, setting out to offer a new agenda for the future shape of a post-1988 religious education in our secondary schools.

It is written in the belief that the future of the subject lies with those who, day after day, year after year, go into the classroom and take on the challenge of teaching religious education at the chalk-face. Genuine curriculum development proceeds from below, not from above. Put another way, this book seeks to take the *professionalism* of teachers with the utmost seriousness. There is a danger that, with a growing emphasis on the importance of classroom skills and effective practice (an importance I would not question for a moment), the art of teaching will somehow become de-professionalized: that we will wake up one day to discover a generation of religious education teachers well trained in the skills of classroom teaching, but lacking in any insight into their professional roles and responsibilities.

Alongside effective teaching skills and pupil management must be found the ability to stand back and take account of the nature of classroom learning and interaction as they relate to the complex and ambiguous question of the nature and purpose of religious education. A professional teacher should be more than an effective practitioner; they should take on board the responsibility of also being a reflective practitioner: one who can fish for themselves.

Consequently the book focuses not so much on classroom practice, as on a reflection on the nature, aims and purposes of that practice. It is probably best read during a school holiday, or in that breathing space once the challenge of teaching practice is over. That, I hope, does not make it an irrelevant academic treatise. I have endeavoured throughout to keep a constant focus on the relevance of the text to the professional needs of classroom teachers.

One work of warning. If the ideas presented in the book were offered in a seminar with a class of students, it would probably be with my tongue firmly in my cheek, and not without a strong hint of irony. Typically, my students would respond with a knowing frown, indicating that they are aware that once again I am trying to 'wind them up'. Though I take seriously most of what I have to say, my desire is not that the suggestions offered here are taken on board

4

hook, line and sinker. On the contrary, I hope the book will challenge teachers to have the courage to think for themselves, to use my (necessarily in the space available) rather sweeping arguments as springboards for the development of their own reflective practice as professional teachers of religious education.

CHAPTER 1

Religious Education in Search of its Soul

The 'Cinderella subject'?

'So you're a teacher then: what is it exactly you teach?'. For many years my stock answer to the question, normally accompanied with a wry smile, was, 'Children'! The reason for this was not, as some might assume, that I had any problem with the fact that my subject specialism was, and remains, religious education. On the contrary, I have always taken great pride in that fact. No, my motivation was that experience had shown that a more direct answer was, more often than not, a guaranteed way of ending the conversation before it had begun. Like it or not, the phrase 'religious education' seemed to make people uncomfortable, to open up a set of issues they would rather leave unexplored.

Did it conjure up in their minds images, possibly drawn from their own classroom experience, that they could not feel at home with? Did it perhaps bring back memories, of an over-heated classroom on a damp and dreary Friday afternoon, with the condensation running down the windows; of a teacher droning on about some apparently utterly irrelevant text from the book of Leviticus; of dog-eared Bibles covered with ink blots and decorated with the occasional obscenity; of interminable hours spent day-dreaming, gazing out of the window, waiting for the bell to ring?

Did it cause them to reconsider their perceptions of me, as if I must somehow be set apart from the norm because I was devoting my professional working life to teaching *that* subject? Was their response governed by an image of a 'typical' religious education teacher: a rather sad-looking, scruffy figure in a tweed jacket, sitting alone in the corner of a staffroom dreading the bell that would call them once again to take part in the futile charade of presenting religion to a group of totally indifferent and disruptive adolescents?

What lies behind such reactions? Why is it that so many people really do not know what to make of religious education? How come the subject has such a dubious status? Is the subject merely a poor relation to those subjects, like English, mathematics and science that enjoy, if not unqualified enthusiasm, then at least a fair measure of prestige and respect? Is it but a mere pretender to those with genuine importance and value? Are the sceptical reactions justified? Is it not simply a fact of life that religious education is irrelevant to our contemporary education system? Or is it possibly, like Cinderella, a sovereign subject, but one for some reason shunned and forced to wear rags and live life as a pauper?

Some may well question this whole characterization: in painting this rather negative picture am I not actually saying more about my own psychological hang-ups than the reality of contemporary religious education? Has not the subject always enjoyed a privileged status in government legislation? Surely the 1944 Education Act made it the only compulsory subject on the curriculum, and was this not reinforced by its designation as *the* basic subject in the curriculum set in place by the 1988 legislation? Is it not being offered as the backbone which must support the rest of the curriculum? Is delivery of the spiritual dimension of education not *the* golden thread that runs throughout recent curriculum innovations? Is there any other subject that is compulsory for all throughout every year of formal schooling? What other subject area is offered a mechanism for curriculum development, support and monitoring so sophisticated and sensitive to local needs? Far from wearing rags, is not the subject already regaled in finery?

A more cynical story can, I would suggest, be narrated from the same set of facts: seeking an easy passage for the Act through Parliament, and mindful of the need to appease both the conservative Christian and the progressive liberal lobbies, whilst at the same time avoiding treading on the toes of leaders of minority religious communities, the government came up with a piece of legislation that was so vague, so open to a variety of interpretations, as to allow it to mean all things to all people. Rather than take the bull by the horns and tackle head-on the issue raised by the complexity and confusion surrounding the subject, ministers chose instead to take the easy way out: to side-step the issues and allow them to be worked through at a local level. Nationally-agreed attainment targets and programmes of study were not to be the stuff religious education is made of: that path had too many pitfalls, risks and challenges to make it politically expedient. This sent a clear message to parents, governors, head teachers and curriculum managers: naturally the subject is important, but perhaps not that important; of course it is one of the compulsory subjects, but just possibly some subjects are more compulsory than others!

Regardless of which of these two stories we prefer, in the cold light of day the fact remains that religious education retains an uncertain, even ambiguous, place in the curriculum. Forced to compete with the claims of subjects within the National Curriculum, it faces a continuous battle for timetable space. It is often found reduced to a token period in the week, or even integrated into broader curriculum areas such as humanities or personal and social education. We have here an example of the reality known in the trade as the 'squeeze syndrome': 'Yes, of course you can teach the subject adequately in 30 minutes a week'. Support and interest is often low: not just amongst the pupils themselves, but also in the attitudes of staff, governors, management and parents. This certainly reflects an uncertainty as to the value of the subject in an increasingly pragmatic and utilitarian education system.

That the 1988 Act left question marks over the nature and status of religious education is a view confirmed by the responses of two key figures given the task of implementing the legislation. John Patten, Secretary of State for Education, and David Pascall, Chair of the National Curriculum Council, both approached their tasks from the perspective of personal commitments to the importance of religious education; both have felt the need to state clearly that the subject must not be allowed to become a poor relation to subjects within the National Curriculum itself; both implicitly have recognized the danger of religious education becoming a 'Cinderella subject'.

All this is not to say that excellence is not to be found; on the contrary there are a vast number of flourishing religious education departments up and down the country. However, all too often such good practice is the result of what might be termed 'curriculum development by personality': good practice rooted in the single-minded skill and enthusiasm of an individual teacher able to generate motivation in the face of a mixture of opposition and apathy, rather than good practice rooted in a school community's unqualified acceptance of the importance and value of the subject.

Regardless of whether one approaches recent developments with an air of enthusiasm or an air of cynicism, the fact remains that all is not perfect in the religious education world. At best its end-of-term report reads: 'Could do better'.

The root of the problem

Why is the situation like it is? I doubt if the blame should be placed on extrinsic causes. There is, it is true, no particular flood of applicants for training in the field; religious education remains, unofficially of course, a shortage subject, and the battle for places on PGCE courses is not a particularly intense one. Nevertheless, the quality of religious education teachers seems to me to be certainly no worse, and in some cases a good deal better, than that available to other subject areas.

In the field of curriculum support, religious education has developed a series of networks second to none. The quality of published material and teaching resources, though patchy, is generally excellent; the work of subject advisors and support staff, and the contribution of resource centres, professional bodies, subject conferences, working parties and the like bear witness to the enthusiasm and complexity of debate surrounding the subject. There seems to be a vigour and enthusiasm that is a reflection of genuine health and growth within religious education itself.

If not then in these areas, where might we look to discover the cause of the rather dubious status of religious education? Is not the root of the problem to be found in an intrinsic cause: the particular problems associated with the subject surely do no more than reflect the fact that religion in contemporary society is itself an ambiguous, confusing and contradictory entity?

As a young student of theology I once spent part of a Christmas vacation sorting mail for the Post Office. The extremely tedious work was made bearable by an on-going conversation I had with one of the regular staff: he refused to accept, point blank, that it was actually possible to study religion at university. There could, he believed, be no intelligent substance to what he saw as essentially outmoded superstition. To claim to study for a degree in theology was for him a contradiction in terms: one might as well claim to be doing a degree in astrology, or produce doctoral research defending the notion of a 'flat earth'. Indeed his assumption was that I was only masquerading as a student, using the cover to supplement my unemployment benefit!

I retell this story because it seems to me to reflect an ambiguity that lies at the very heart of religious questions and religious beliefs, and hence also at the very heart of the enterprise of teaching religious education. Does religion stand at the centre of our understanding of our humanity, of our society, of the ultimate questions of purpose, meaning and truth that the universe forces upon us? Or is it a mere irrelevance, a superstitious remnant of a past age that the intelligent and sophisticated have outgrown, but which the timid and frightened continue to cling to in the way a drowning individual grabs a life line?

This ambiguity is rooted, in the west, in the fall-out from the age of the Enlightenment: that period in western cultural and intellectual history in which, so one telling of its history relates, humanity came of age, threw off the shackles of religious belief and had the courage to trust its own reason. Theology was replaced by humanism, the churches began to lose their grip on the hearts and minds of the people of Europe, and a journey of emancipation along the path towards atheism, agnosticism and secularism began.

Religious belief, of course, did not disappear following the Enlightenment, but it was certainly shifted from centre stage. The importance and truth of religious belief was no longer something that could be taken for granted: it needed to justify itself, explain itself to its 'cultured despisers' (to borrow a phrase from the theologian Schleiermacher). For many this task was too challenging to contemplate. It was a far easier option to retreat behind the protective walls of a religious community, to refuse to address the challenges of rationalism and secularization. Hence the growth of the phenomena of 'fundamentalism', and the consequent misuse of the word to label all who take religious belief with any seriousness.

Further confusion was added to the religious map with the growth of contact, through exploration, colonial expansion and increasingly sophisticated methods of travel and communication, with a whole host of non-Christian religious belief systems. The reality of religious pluralism was one that could no longer be ignored: no longer could Christian Europe patronize Jews and label Muslims as 'infidels' existing on the fringes of civilisation. Religious belief becomes even more ambiguous when it is realized that there is a whole host of religious traditions to choose between.

The growth of secularism, the development of religious fundamentalism and the acknowledgement of religious pluralism combined to create the current reality of religious ambiguity. It gave birth to the enormous variety of beliefs and to the extremes of commitment and rejection that mark the position of religion in western civilisation in the late twentieth century. If religion is indeed no more than an outmoded superstition, then a secular rather than religious foundation for our existence is presumably the only viable option available. If, on the other hand, religion is actually close to the heart of reality, then which religious system do we opt for in the face of the diverse options available to us in our modern western culture?

In the face of these issues of pluralism, fundamentalism and secularism it becomes easier to see why individuals might find themselves uncomfortable with religious education. Religion lacks the universal public acceptance that other subjects enjoy. It leads us paradoxically into the realms of both uncertainty and truth, whilst at the same time nurturing both cynicism and apathy, faith and commitment. Wishing to hold fast to one's own response and solutions to these issues, understandably perhaps one may become wary of this position becoming undermined in the classroom by teachers who have themselves developed other solutions. Whichever version of the religious story is told in the classroom, there will always be those who would wish an alternative story to be taught to our children. Little wonder that the charge of 'indoctrination' seems to be waiting in the wings ready to ambush teachers whichever way they turn.

In other words, the ambiguity of religion in society creates a climate of suspicion that surrounds religious education. It is this reality that forms the single major factor holding back the subject. The controversial nature of religion hangs like a shadow over our classrooms. May Cinderella go to the ball? Will the slipper fit? Is religious education the stuff of princesses or paupers?

Selling the birthright

Our modern age remains firmly under the spell of Descartes, a key figure in the Enlightenment, and one often referred to as the 'founder of modern philosophy'. His thoughts embodied the human desire and need for clarity and certainty in our knowledge and life-style. He offered us an image of a drowning man, unable to place his feet on the bottom of the stream or lift his head above water, a man desperate for safety, security, certainty and firm foundations. For many, such foundations could no longer be provided by the essentially ambiguous reality of religious belief.

Recently an alternative possibility has emerged in western thought as western culture moves from a modern to a post-modern understanding of our world. Philosophers such as Wittgenstein have drawn attention to the limitations of human reason and the security it claims to provide. The true nature of the universe and of our place within it is essentially mysterious, always one step beyond the ability of human reason to comprehend it. This forces us into an ambiguous situation that should be welcomed and embraced. The more we claim to know the 'answers', the more narrow-minded and blinkered we become. The more we are attuned to the complexities of reality, the more aware of the contingency and provisionality of our understanding, then the more our minds become open to new possibilities, to deeper and more profound truth. The Greek philosopher Socrates was in tune with this approach to human understanding many centuries ago when he offered the world the apparently paradoxical suggestion that the wise person is the one most aware of their own ignorance.

This dispute about the nature of human understanding offers a challenge to religious education, operating as it must do at present in a climate of suspicion. The challenge is in the form of a choice between two options, two ways forward: the broad straight road or the narrow winding lane. The former offers the certainty of immediate gratification and safety, the latter the possibility of long-term fulfilment, but at the risk of confusion and consternation.

Contemporary religious education, I suggest, has opted for the former. Like Esau selling his birthright, or Faust his soul to the devil, it takes the easy most immediate route. Given the ambiguity of religion, the most effective way of justifying the place of the subject in the curriculum is to redefine religion into something that can be acceptable to modern society. Religion is thus pre-packaged, its rough edges shorn off and smoothed over, its contradictions and obscurities hidden away. It is turned into an entity defined in such a way as to be safe, secure, neutral. This is essentially a policy of appeasement, of swimming with the tide, producing a subject for all seasons.

This policy has been achieved at an enormous cost. Put bluntly, the process of denying the ambiguity of religion denies pupils access to any depth of understanding of the complexity and ambiguity of our diverse religious and areligious heritage, it denies them the right to wrestle with the issues for themselves. Above all, it sidesteps the issue of the truth of religious and non-religious beliefs. To repeat our earlier question: is religion, and if so which particular form of religion, at the heart of the questions of truth and meaning that our existence in the universe forces upon us, or is it mere outmoded superstition? The ambiguity of this question, the fact that there are no clear answers, should not delude us into thinking that the question itself is of no value. On the contrary, the question, regardless of the answer given, is of vital importance, constituting the heart and soul of claims and counter-claims of atheists, agnostics and theists.

Religious education has, with a few noble exceptions, chosen not to follow the narrow path that offers a pilgrimage through the ambiguous terrain of the question of religious truth. The safer option is to sidestep the whole question, to present religion in a watered-down, secure form, that challenges nobody and hence has nothing worth saying. Our age turns the wine of ambiguity into the water of false security, breeding in the process generations of religious illiterates. We produce contented pigs when we should be nurturing discontented philosophers. Such is the heart of the argument of this book.

CHAPTER 2

Perspectives on Contemporary Religious Education

Religious education after the 1988 Act

At present the dust is still settling following the introduction of the 1988 Education Reform Act, a piece of legislation that fundamentally changed the nature of education in England and Wales. It is difficult at this stage to get a clear picture of all the implications of the new legislation: we are still too close to it chronologically, and the practical changes it has brought about are only now falling into place in schools and classrooms.

A deputy head once remarked to me that she and her colleagues valued students coming into their school if for no other reason than that they could shed light on current developments. As newcomers to the profession, they were able to assimilate these far more quickly than experienced teachers who for years had become used to working within a very different framework. An exaggeration, I am sure, but in a climate of rapid (some would say far too rapid) change, one can see the point being made.

How is religious education shaping up in a post-1988 education climate? What issues and approaches are central to its agenda? We will attempt to answer these questions in a number of ways: by looking at the development of the subject between 1944 and 1988; by outlining the provisions of the 1988 Act regarding religious education and school worship; by outlining the views of key groups lobbying over the future of the subject; and by describing a set of key issues that are central to contemporary debate.

Religious education 1944-1988

The 'ploughman's lunch', served in pubs up and down the country, offers a cheap, nutritious, easily prepared meal that draws on a tradition of British culture that can be traced back to the good old days, to an age when Constable painted the countryside and tarmac and tractors had not yet been invented. Such fare fits in well with the 'traditional' image that many public houses seek to nurture. The stark reality of course is that those 'good old days' never happened: the picture of ploughmen sitting on the edge of a field tucking into bread, cheese, salad and a pint is the invention of twentieth century market researchers.

In 1944, politicians, church leaders and educationalists, faced with the challenge of redrawing the framework of education in England and Wales, drew on a story similar in form to that of the 'ploughman's lunch' myth. The story went something like this: in the good old days Britain had been a Christian country, a country in cultural, moral, social and economic terms at the centre of the 'civilized' world. Through colonialism and missionary activity she had spread her civilization to the far corners of the globe, greatly enriching humanity in the process.

However, at some stage, so the myth goes, things began to go wrong: somehow the nation, along with the rest of civilized Europe, wandered from its garden of Eden. Exactly when and how might be unclear; nevertheless the warning signs were there for all to see amidst the mud and horror of the Great War of 1914-18. Though society in the 1920s and 1930s surrounded itself with frivolity and hid its face from reality, by 1944 the stark truth of a European civilization that was sick to the core now had to be faced up to. To do otherwise was impossible as newsreels brought to cinemas in towns and villages the length and breadth of the country horrific images of Auschwitz, Belsen and other extermination camps, and of the aftermath of the bombing of Dresden and other German cities. Hiroshima and Nagasaki were, of course, just around the corner.

The 1944 Education Act was the product of a wartime coalition government. With the war in Europe won, attention could be paid to reconstruction, a reconstruction rooted in the need to bring healing to a sick Europe through its moral and spiritual rejuvenation. Education was to play a major role in this process. The legislation offered a blueprint for the rebirth of a nation emerging from the chaos of armed conflict — a blueprint for a new national order that looked backwards for its source and inspiration to Britain's mythical past. It sought to re-establish that golden age, lost in the folly of the twentieth century, when Christianity provided the moral and spiritual backbone of the country.

The confessional *model*

Under the 1944 Act religious education was to be the one compulsory subject on the curriculum. It was to aim at the instruction of the children in the Christian faith, an instruction to be reinforced by a daily act of collective worship. By teaching Christianity in a nurturing environment, the central values of the faith would, so it was hoped, become embedded in the hearts and minds of the nation's youth, thus bringing about a moral regeneration that would form the heart and soul of the country's recovery.

The legal framework gave support to a *confessional* form of religious education, rooted in study of the Bible and with an emphasis on those Biblical texts (the ten commandments, the sermon on the mount, etc.) that could provide a morally uplifting framework on which children could ground their lives. This *confessional* religious education was to be supported and nurtured by a daily act of Christian worship in schools.

The implicit *model*

By the early 1960s the idealism of the myth of 'Christian Britain' had begun to wane. The fact that the authority and teaching of the church no longer went unchallenged, and for many was increasingly irrelevant to their lives, was beginning to be recognized. The realization was dawning that Britain was essentially a post-Christian society: regular church-going had plummeted to new lows; the Church of England seemed to many to be little more than an appendage to the civic life of the nation; the Christian Gospel had become reduced to a type of post-Christian 'folk religion' offering access to the traditional 'rites of passage' (baptisms, marriages, funerals) for those who required them, regardless of personal belief or commitment. These moves towards a secular society were of course not new, though perhaps for the first time they had reached the public consciousness. As we have seen, they could be traced back at least 300 years to the 'Enlightenment', that revolution in science, philosophy and culture that had ushered in our current 'modern' era. Suddenly the belief that education could overturn years of profound cultural change simply by making religious education compulsory appeared naive in the extreme.

Teachers of religious education recognized this more quickly than most, faced as they were with increasingly vocal expressions of the 'irrelevance' of learning the Bible coming from pupils in the classroom. Their reaction though was not to develop a religious education that responded realistically to these changes in society, rather it sought ways of making *confessionalism* more effective. Thus the 1960s saw the rise of an *implicit* model of religious education that sought to achieve the same aims, of induction and nurture in a Christian faith and value system as the *confessional* model. The difference was that by starting, not from Christian belief itself, but from the pupils' own perspectives, *implicit* religious education could kick-start the stalled process of a religious education for moral rejuvenation.

This 'pupil perspective' was understood in terms of children's moral questions and uncertainties, their aesthetic experience of the wonders of human life and of nature, and the 'existential' issues they faced concerning the purpose and meaning of their existence. By starting from, and taking account of, children's own perspectives, religious educators sought to build a bridge that would lead them to a new and valid understanding of the Christian faith. If lessons now started with discussions about family life, poverty, sex, drugs, or even, for the more adventurous and streetwise teacher, 'rock and roll', the ultimate aim for the subject remained firmly in place. The task was still that of getting back to the Bible and its teaching.

The explicit/phenomenological *model*

For at least four groups this approach of *confessionalism,* or of the neo-confessionalism of the *implicit* model, was unacceptable in a modern, open society.

Humanists pointed out that the beliefs of Christianity, and the assumption that morality needed a specifically religious foundation, had become matters of fundamental dispute. It was perfectly possible, they suggested, to live a basically good and virtuous life without any recourse to religious belief. To instruct children in such a way that ignored these facts was tantamount to indoctrination.

Adherents of other non-Christian faith systems asked why children should not have the right to learn about other religious traditions. The existence of non-Christian religious communities could of course be traced back in British history to before the advent of Christianity itself. Now the growth of immigration in the 1950s and 1960s both expanded the communities already in place and added new ones to an increasingly pluralist society. Racial violence, spurred on by politicians warning of 'rivers of blood' on the streets and linked to the growth of fascism on the extreme right wing of British politics, created an environment in which minority communities, many of whom had previously been content to enrich society in a passive, quietist manner, discovered the need to articulate and defend their needs and aspirations.

Educationalists pointed out that the form of instruction envisaged by the 1944 Act led not to education but to forms of religious nurture, and asked whether 'education' rather than 'nurture' was not a more appropriate way for schools to go about their business. Was there not a fundamental difference between instruction *in* Christianity and education *about* religion?

For some Christians grave doubts were expressed about the adequacy of the *confessional* and *implicit* approaches. Was there not a danger in confusing church with school? Was not the Gospel that proclaimed human freedom compromised by being forced upon children in such a manner? Did the educational system not confuse 'Christianity' with 'Christendom'?

The result of these series of questions was a fundamental shift in the structure of religious education from a traditional Christian to a liberal model. For the first time the reality of the true nature of British society was taken seriously. How could the subject respond to the demands of a modern secular, pluralistic world? What could replace the confessional approach, now that the myth of the golden age of Christian Britain had been recognized for what it was? A way forward was to be found in the wording of the 1944 Act: it had used the word 'religious' throughout, though the assumption had been made that it was synonymous with 'Christian'. Here, inadvertently, was a loophole worth both exploring and exploiting.

The lead in this shift to a liberal form of religious education was given by the Birmingham Agreed Syllabus of 1975. Alongside Christianity were placed a variety of other 'life stances', including not only other key religions (Judaism, Islam, Hinduism, Buddhism, etc.) but also the secular alternatives of Humanism and Marxism. With the new liberal content came a new liberal aim: no longer concerned with instilling in pupils a confession of the Christian faith, the purpose of religious education was now to bring about an understanding of a variety of belief systems, rather than commitment to one.

In all of this, the original concern with moral and spiritual development was not lost. However, from a liberal perspective it would now be brought about not through a return to Christian confession but through the growth of a harmonious multicultural society in which different traditions are understood and respected. This liberal approach to religious education that grew up in the 1970s and was consolidated in the 1980s was referred to as the *explicit/phenomenological* model; 'explicit' to contrast it with the prevailing *implicit* model, 'phenomenological' in recognition of its concern with the outward cultural phenomena of the various religious traditions.

The spiritual *model*

Towards the end of the 1980s the liberal approach began to develop a concern with the spiritual development of children, and a fourth model, that of *spiritual* religious education, or education in *spirituality* began to develop. Just as the *implicit* model had attempted to go beyond *confessionalism* by trying to draw out the relevance of Christianity through starting from the pupils' own perspectives, so now the *spiritual* model set out to go beyond the limitations of the *explicit/phenomenological* model by drawing out the relevance of religious traditions to individual and social life by starting from the spiritual experience and concerns of children. Needless to say, 'spirituality' was understood in a broad humanistic sense, and in no way was it equated with education into an exclusively Christian spirituality.

The period 1944-1988 thus marked a fundamental revolution in religious education in the form of a shift from a 'closed' Christian agenda to an 'open' liberal one. Interestingly, though, both the Christian and liberal approaches moved through parallel stages of development. Both started from the objective reality of religion and religious traditions in society, both came face-to-face with the question of the relevance of this tradition, and both responded to this challenge by turning inwards, towards the subjective experience of children as a starting point for religious education, in the belief that such a process would enable them to appropriate religious traditions in more meaningful and relevant ways. This process tended to locate the 'problem' of religious education in the subjective perceptions of pupils, rather than in the ambiguity of religion itself. It was into this situation that the 1988 Education Reform Act was thrust.

Provisions of the 1988 Act

Where the 1944 Act had focused control of education on the local education authorities (LEAs), the 1988 legislation saw the polarization of this control. On the one hand, local management of schools (LMS), and the option of opting out of LEA control by choosing grant maintained status (GMS), gave individual schools greater freedom to develop their own identity and ethos, and greater control over the management of their own affairs and education provision. This process was furthered by the establishment of City Technology Colleges (CTCs), which introduced into education the notion of specialist schools with expertise in, and concentration on, a particular area of the curriculum. On the other hand, power also moved from local to national level. Here leadership from the centre could guide individual schools towards good practice by setting an agenda via control of the newly-introduced National Curriculum, and oversight of procedures for the assessment of pupils' and schools' achievements. Schools thus gained freedom, but were to be held accountable for the way in which they used their new powers.

The jewel in the crown of the 1988 Act was the National Curriculum. It comprised ten foundation subjects: three core subjects (English, mathematics and science) and seven other foundation subjects (technology, history, geography, music, art, physical education and, at secondary level, a modern foreign language). Statutory Instruments (or 'Orders') are used to set out, and when necessary revise, the programmes of study, attainment targets and assessment procedures of each subject within the National Curriculum. The Secretary of State for Education, responsible for these Instruments, can draw on non-statutory guidance from the National Curriculum Council (NCC) and the School Examinations and Assessment Council (SEAC). At the time of writing these two bodies are due to be merged to form the Schools Curriculum and Assessment Authority.

The National Curriculum is to be seen as no more than part of the 'whole curriculum', which includes all other work done in schools: other subject areas, and cross-curricular themes such as literacy, numeracy, careers education, gender and multicultural issues. While these form an essential part of the whole curriculum, they are not legislated for in the way in which National Curriculum subjects are.

The whole curriculum must provide each pupil's entitlement to a broadly-based and balanced learning experience that fulfils the fundamental aims of education as set out in the Act. Schools must offer a curriculum that

> promotes the spiritual, moral, cultural, mental and physical development of pupils at the school and of society; and prepares such pupils for the opportunities, responsibilities and experiences of adult life (DES, 1988, Section 1, 2).

And what of religious education? The 1988 Act presents its religious clauses in the form of amendments to the 1944 legislation. The religious content of the Act outlines the scope of the legislation and the various contexts in which it operates, distinguishes between 'religious education' and 'collective worship' and describes the required provision for each, and requires all local authorities to establish Standing Advisory Councils on Religious Education (SACREs).

Scope and context

All schools in the maintained sector, including sixth-form colleges, must provide religious education and collective worship (the only exception being special schools, for which separate arrangements are made). All schools in the voluntary sector, namely schools with a religious foundation, mostly Anglican, Roman Catholic and Jewish (frequently referred to as 'denominational' or 'church' schools), are free to provide religious education in a form that reflects their particular faith tradition, following the direction of their governing body in accordance with the school's trust deeds. County schools (often referred to as 'state' schools to distinguish them from 'church' schools) must work within the framework provided for them by the local SACRE. Grant-maintained schools must offer religious education in accordance with one of the locally agreed syllabuses, though not necessarily that adopted by their old local authority.

For those who do not wish their children to take part in either religious education or collective worship there is a right of withdrawal. In the same way, safeguards exist for teachers who do not wish to participate in collective worship or teach religious education. Withdrawal by either pupil or staff remains relatively rare, and is unlikely to be an issue within a voluntary school since full participation in collective worship and religious education is likely to be a condition of entry to the school.

Apart from those pupils who are withdrawn by parents, religious education and collective worship must be provided for all pupils registered in a school. Unlike the National Curriculum which applies only to students of compulsory school age, the provisions on religious education and worship apply to all post-16 pupils whether in schools or sixth-form colleges.

Religious education

The National Curriculum together with religious education form the 'basic curriculum' which all schools must provide. The subject thus has a special status: of equal standing with foundation subjects, but without nationally prescribed attainment targets, programmes of study and assessment arrangements. The curriculum for county schools is to be prescribed at local level in the form of agreed syllabuses by SACREs which may, if they choose, draw on advice from the NCC. If a SACRE chooses, it may adopt the same format of attainment targets, programmes of study and assessment arrangements as those in place for foundation subjects.

New locally agreed syllabuses must,

> reflect the fact that religious traditions in Great Britain are in the main Christian whilst taking account of the teaching and practices of the other principal religions represented in Great Britain (DES, 1988, Section 8,3).

The subject must be 'non-denominational' that is, not use a form or style of teaching rooted in a particular religious tradition, though teaching about denominational differences is permitted.

Collective worship

In both county and voluntary schools there must be a daily act of collective worship for all pupils. It may be organized for separate groups of pupils and take place at any time during the school day. While voluntary schools are free to decide on the nature of collective worship themselves, in county schools worship must be 'wholly or mainly of a broadly Christian character', though 'without being distinctive of any particular denomination' (DES, 1988, Section 7, 1 and 2). The implication of this seems to be that at least the majority of acts of worship in a school term must be broadly Christian in character, though what precisely this means remains unclear. Is, for example a 'thought for the day' type of reflection on the theme of 'respect for others' Christian enough, and does it constitute worship? On top of all this, what might the 49 per cent of assemblies that need not have a broadly based Christian character look like?

22

Such acts of worship must be appropriate to the family background, ages and aptitudes of the pupils. While the latter two requirements merely seem to state the obvious (is any school likely to put on an act of collective worship inappropriate to the ages and aptitudes of pupils? But then again . . . !), the former asks the question of the position of pupils whose backgrounds lie in non-Christian religious traditions but who have not been opted-out of the requirement for collective worship. In this situation the headteacher may apply to the SACRE for a determination that the requirement for collective Christian worship should not apply, either to the school as a whole or to a particular group of pupils within the school.

SACREs

Local SACREs, which held an advisory and optional role under the 1944 legislation, must now be set up by each local authority. A SACRE is constituted by four groups, representing: i) Christian and other religious groups that reflect the principal religious traditions within the boundaries of the LEA; ii) the Church of England; iii) teachers' associations; iv) the LEA. Their principal role is:

> to advise the authority upon such matters connected with religious worship in county schools and the religious education to be given in accordance with an agreed syllabus as the authority may refer to the council or as the council may see fit (DES, 1988, Section 11.1)

In practice this involves the SACRE in: the revision and development of the current agreed syllabus; determining if a headteacher's application for exemption from the requirements of collective worship are appropriate and admissible; reviewing the existing provision for religious education in schools and advising on issues such as teaching methods, teaching material and teacher training; supporting the complaints machinery built into the 1988 Act in so far as it relates to issues of religion, when and if the LEA asks for such help; and publishing an annual report on its work.

The current agenda

In retrospect the religious clauses of the 1988 Education Reform Act take on something of an enigmatic character. The importance of religious education is stressed, yet is not to be part of the National Curriculum. The language of 'education' replaces the language of 'instruction' found in the 1944 Act, yet the retention of collective worship still hints at a nurturing and instructional model of the learning process. The content is to be 'in the main Christian', yet other world religions must be included in syllabuses.

The clue to unravelling the enigma lies, I believe, in the political context and the compromise sought by ministers as a result of this. In the initial discussion surrounding the proposed National Curriculum, little mention was made of religious education, short of the fact that it was already legislated for under the 1944 Act and hence needed no further attention. The combination of lack of personal interest in the area amongst certain ministers, combined with the respect for the age-old advice to let sleeping dogs lie, might have led to matters being left there had it not had been for intense lobbying from a number of interested groupings. Three of these continue to play central roles in contemporary debate.

The conservative lobby

In the political environment of the late 1980s, with its rhetoric of a return to traditional values and attitudes, there were those on the conservative wing of British politics who proclaimed, with renewed vigour, the central place of Christianity in the nation's cultural heritage, and hence the need for it to be given a pivotal role in the country's education system. The then Prime Minister played her part in encouraging this debate, supported by the Centre for Policy Studies and other organizations. One result, at least at a popular level, was the re-introduction to educational circles of the debates surrounding the issue of confessionalism and a religiously-rooted education system.

The liberal lobby

On the other side of the coin stood those whose vision was of education for a harmonious multicultural society; for a society rooted in the rhetoric of tolerance and equality; for a society in which diversity was an enriching experience. The possibility of a return to a Christian imperialism was to viewed with the utmost suspicion, and the positive gains of the 1970s and early 1980s needed protection and consolidation in the face of the perceived conservative threat.

The faith-communities lobby

At the same time, adherents of a variety of world faiths asked no more than the right and freedom to educate the children of their community in its faith and traditions, regardless of the outcome of the liberal-conservative debate. Most visibly at the forefront stood the Muslim community, spurred on by the need to both protect and enrich its communal and religious life in the face of pressures from a secular environment, and quite legitimately anxious to counter a discriminatory education system that denied them the same access to state funding enjoyed by the Christian and Jewish communities. The lead given by the Muslims was taken up by other faith communities including, interestingly enough, significant groups within the various Christian denominations.

The Act itself, by refusing a place for the subject on the National Curriculum and instead offering local control of the curriculum, managed to avoid a national debate that went beyond the language of appeasement and compromise. There was something on offer for all three major lobbies: the centrality of Christianity for the conservatives, the requirement that world religions be taught for the liberals, and the hint that the development of grant-maintained schools may offer a route towards the reality of state-funded Muslim schools for those concerned with the rights of minority religious communities.

Issues and disputes

If we accept that openness and intensity of debate is a sign both of continued interest and concern for the subject, then religious education could be said to be in good health. Not so much the positive result of the requirements of the 1988 Act, rather the result of a political compromise that offers a framework open to further interpretation, development and growth. What issues of debate between the conservative, liberal and faith-focused lobbies are on the current agenda? What issues are likely to be instrumental in the future development of the subject?

Why teach religious education?

The concern for the moral and spiritual rejuvenation of the country is still firmly in place; religious education is still envisaged as in some way playing a major contribution in providing the cement that will hold society together in some sort of moral consensus. The dispute is over the constituency of that cement.

For the liberal lobby the aim of religious education remains that of bringing about an understanding of and empathy with the diversity of religious systems in such a way that mutual respect and toleration will unite a pluralistic society. For members of the conservative lobby this seems all too vague and idealistic: for them society needs a far more concrete value system, a far more explicit distinction between right and wrong, and this is provided for us by the Christian heritage of the nation, a heritage that we must reclaim as our own. It is not always clear here, however, whether this process should involve a retention of the Christian *belief system,* or merely an appropriation of Christian *ethical norms* abstracted from the doctrines.

For adherents of other faiths the issue is a far more basic one. Their concern is to bring up their own children according to the doctrines of their particular faith systems, whilst at the same time allowing those outside access to a deeper understanding of their beliefs. To this end they look for a religious education that does justice to the core of their religions' truth claims rather than one that reduces them to little more than an example of human culture.

Christianity and/or world faiths?

While the Act calls for a balance between Christianity and other principal world faiths, with an acknowledgement that Christianity forms the core of the nation's religious heritage, the exact nature of this balance is a matter of dispute.

The liberals seek to focus on the cultural heritage of the various religious traditions, and seek to find a balance in favour of Christianity being seen as part of the plurality of modern culture. Their emphasis tends to be on exploring religious culture rather than issues of theology and truth, seeing the latter as having the potential to reinforce differences and thus promote intolerance.

The conservatives and faith communities may differ about the proportion of time spent studying religion, but tend to discover common ground in arguing that the subject takes more account of the fundamental theological questions that religious traditions adhere to. A favourite game amongst those cynical about liberal-inspired agreed syllabuses is to search them with a fine-tooth comb for references to the word 'God' amongst phenomenological descriptions of religious clothing, rites of passage and places of worship.

Is school worship part of education?

Within the legal framework of the Act the answer to this question is clearly 'Yes', but its open-ended nature offers scope for a broad range of interpretations. Religious worship can easily be reduced to some form of time for moral reflection, its theological focus turned to a humanistic celebration of the richness and diversity of the traditions that make up a school community. Again, the various lobbies will have opinions on this that do not need to be stated.

This opens up a broader issue, of the relationship between worship and education. How far should worship play an educational role, supporting and enhancing the academic work of the religious education department? Alternatively, how far should worship play a social role, nurturing and reinforcing the school's community and ethos, as a kind of prelude that sets the right conditions in which learning can take place? (For a full discussion of this issue, albeit in the context of primary education, it is well worth looking at Elaine McCreery's *Worship in the Primary School* (1993) in the same series as the present book).

A place for 'church' schools?

As religious education adopted a liberal agenda in the 1970s it was common to hear attacks on religious schools on the grounds that they are socially devisive. By isolating believers from their peers from other traditions, by denying them access to one another, the claim was that prejudice and misunderstandings are reinforced. The dual system of Catholic and Protestant schooling in Northern Ireland was held out as a warning of the consequences of religious schools.

Recent legislation has shifted the focus of the debate. The possibility of schools 'opting out' of LEA control and taking responsibility for their own strategic development has enhanced the notion of the individuality of schools, each with their own particular intake, ethos and aims developed within the framework of the National Curriculum. Such a notion has contributed to the renewed legitimation of religiously-based schools, a fact reflected in the increasingly vocal lobby, which we referred to earlier, for state funding for Muslim schools on the same basis as that offered to the Christian and Jewish communities.

An unresolved issue in this new situation, indeed one of enormous contention within faith communities sponsoring voluntary schools, is that of the formal relationship between opted-out religious schools, in theory now autonomous entities, and their faith communities. It has been suggested that such independence might ultimately reduce a school's religious nature, given the severance of formal links with the religious community and a reliance on funding purely from the public purse.

Neutrality or commitment in the classroom?

During a popular current affairs television programme transmitted recently, the presenter, Kilroy-Silk, was unable to hide his incredulity when faced with a teacher of religious education in the audience who professed herself to be an atheist. His own agenda (whether it was a personal one or one adopted for the sake of bringing life to the debate, it was difficult to tell) was that to teach religious education surely demanded some kind of religious faith, if not in Christianity then at the very least in some other religious system.

Where confessionalism demanded a Christian commitment on the part of the teacher, liberal religious education demanded at the very least a working commitment to religious neutrality. This latter approach was linked with an approach to the teaching of moral education, developed by Stenhouse and others, that stressed the freedom of students to develop their own responses to controversial issues, and gave the teacher the role of a neutral arbiter between classroom disputes. There is now an increasing recognition that such a neutral stance itself involved a value judgement, in terms of an acceptance of the importance of a working neutrality and the ability of individuals to develop adequate moral responses on the basis of their own perspectives. Hence it seems that we encounter a form of commitment on *both* sides of the argument. Both models demand some form of 'commitment': to claim to be religiously neutral is to claim commitment to the acceptance of the equality of the world's religions.

The debate, though still flourishing, has moved on beyond the simply either/or of Christian commitment versus neutrality. If the teacher is concerned with education rather than indoctrination then the issue of the quality of the learning process itself may be seen as taking precedence over the inculcation of a particular belief system. However, the question of how this is to be done, given that any form of education will at least implicitly embody a set of values, remains an unresolved one.

A 'child-centred' religious education?

Both the confessional and liberal models shifted from a focus on 'religion' to a focus on the pupil's own 'religious development'. The language of 'explicit' and 'implicit' forms of religious education reflects a tension that continues to dominate curriculum development in the subject. Is the primary aim of the subject to bring about an objective understanding of religion, or a subjective understanding of an individual's own religious beliefs and attitudes? The danger of the former is often described in terms of the perceived 'irrelevance' of religion to personal development; of the latter, the possibility of a religious education devoid of specifically 'religious' content.

This dilemma reflects the reality that for many pupils there is a gulf between their own personal lives and the beliefs and claims of religion. The question of how to reconcile these two different ways into the subject remains firmly on the agenda.

Is religious education an end in itself?

Finally, in our survey of current issues in religious education, we turn again to the central issue of the fundamental aims of the subject. For many the study of religion is an end in itself: the questions of religious truth and belief contain intrinsic value and importance, and require no further justification. This position may be seen as a development of the confessional model, only here the question of religious truth is approached in a pluralistic rather than purely Christian context. On a Friday night one person goes to the Mosque to pray; on Sunday morning someone goes to church to worship God, while another chooses to wash the car. While all these actions reflect a set of commitments and beliefs sincerely held by those involved, they cannot all be right: someone here must be 'reading' the world wrongly, must be basing their lives on false premises. Hence the educated exploration of the issues is seen as important and valuable in itself.

An alternative approach to the subject starts by suspending the question of religious truth: in a pluralistic society we are free to believe whatever we wish, provided it has no negative consequences for others. The role of religious education is not to explore this issue, but to look at the way religion may enhance the smooth working of such a multicultural society. Religious education here is not so much an end in itself as a means to bring about tolerance, mutual understanding and more effective ways of enabling diverse groups to live together in modern Britain.

Like the other issues outlined above, there is no consensus as to any possible solution of the dilemmas they raise. They are offered here, albeit too briefly, as a way of introducing current debate, of highlighting the disputes that form the cutting edge of the development of the subject. It has been argued that the Act offers a basic framework and structure, but leaves open the question of the precise nature of the actual content, process and aims of the subject. If we view this situation, not negatively from a perspective of any perceived failure on the part of the legislation, but positively as a golden opportunity to take the process of curriculum development in religious education a stage further, then inevitably we must look to the future. In which direction, given the current disputes and controversy, lies the path forwards towards a viable religious education for the 1990s? Might it be a path that allows the subject to rediscover its soul?

CHAPTER 3

Towards a New Agenda

The current crossroads

As we saw in the previous chapter, the 1988 Education Reform Act has once again placed the question of the nature of religious education in the melting pot. Within the framework of the new legislation there is scope for exploring a number of possible ways forward. The popular media has, not unexpectedly, chosen to stereotype the debate regarding the future development of religious education. It is presented in the simplistic terms of a choice between a renewed confessionalism or a resurgent liberalism.

On 21 December 1992, the *Daily Express* ran a brief story headlined, 'Carols out of tune in schools'. In it we were told that 'Christmas carols could be doctored in schools for fear of upsetting Muslim pupils'. Apparently, religious education advisers wanted reference to the birth of Jesus removed from carols in schools, and indeed the paper was able to report that 'some multi-faith schools have already adopted the "politically correct" carols'. Reacting against this threat of a resurgent liberalism, the Conservative member of Parliament Geoffrey Dickens was quoted as saying:

> People of other religions celebrate their own festivals — why should we be stopped from celebrating ours?... I don't see why we should have other religions imposed on us. It is dreadful this mad scheme has been allowed to get so far.

The implications of the news report seem clear: either religious education chooses the liberal line of adopting a neutral and balanced attitude towards world faiths, treading the tightrope of avoiding saying anything that might possibly upset anybody, or else it chooses to back a renewed acceptance of the nation's 'Christian heritage'.

The specialist media has, perhaps more surprisingly, tended to portray a similarly stereotyped picture of the debate. The *Times Educational Supplement* led its Christmas day edition in 1992 with the headline 'Schools defy Tory Christian crusade'. We learn that,

> Britain's Christian traditions are being ignored in schools... according to a TES survey published today. The survey of more than 100 primary and secondary schools, suggests many are flouting the Government's wish to reinforce Christian values in religious education lessons and through a daily act of collective worship.

A secondary head teacher is reported as saying 'I don't think this... is feasible or advisable in our multi-ethnic society'. What is of interest here is the terms in which the survey is reported. We are offered the same either/or by the *Times Educational Supplement* as we were by the *Daily Express,* a straight choice between a renewed Christian confessional and a resurgent multicultural liberalism.

Both confessionalism and liberalism tend to take as their starting point the desire to introduce pupils into a viable and coherent value system. This desire to ground religious education in the search for a cement that is able to bind together a diverse and fragmented society takes precedence over a concern for academic study of religion as an end in itself. Where confessionalism and liberalism differ, despite this common agenda, is in their understanding of exactly which moral value system pupils should be inducted into.

Confessionalism tends to see the diversity of our contemporary pluralistic society as a problem to be overcome. Such diversity, it is argued, leads to moral relativism, confusion and an ill-disciplined freedom. The way forward is through a return to a basic set of common standards and values. Hence confessionalism invokes the myth of the golden age of Christian Britain. It assumes that by once again placing Christianity at the centre of religious education, schools will be able to draw on Christian values in order to counteract what is perceived as the moral and spiritual vacuum in the nation.

In contrast, liberalism tends to see the diversity of our contemporary pluralistic society as an opportunity to be embraced and welcomed. Only by recognizing, tolerating and respecting this diversity can the values and moral standards of society hope to move forward. Such a diversity of values and culture, so the argument runs, can only serve to enrich and deepen the life of the nation. Hence liberalism invokes a vision of a flourishing, prejudice-free multicultural society. The study of religious culture is here seen as a key factor in the task of inducting pupils into the core values of openness and tolerance.

I would like to suggest in this chapter that both of these two popular options are in reality dead ends, that each contains fundamental flaws that cannot be overcome. We need to look at the issues from a different perspective, to move towards developing a new agenda for the subject, one that looks beyond the cul-de-sacs of liberalism and confessionalism.

A renewed confessionalism

What then are the fundamental flaws in the programme of a 'renewed confessionalism', the attempt to place Britain's 'Christian heritage' once again at the centre of the religious education curriculum? We can deal with objections to this programme fairly briefly, since they were touched upon in the last chapter.

First, although Christianity remains the official state religion, the reality is that secularization has led to Christianity, as a living religion, playing little more than a marginal role in the life of the country. Agnosticism, and to a lesser extent atheism, have become common responses to the truth claims of Christianity. To claim that Britain is a 'Christian' country is to fail to distinguish between Christian faith and the vestiges of Christian religion in the civic and social life of the population.

Second, to place Christianity at the centre fails to do justice to the multi-faith nature of society. It is doubtful whether an education that ignores the truth claims of other major world religions apart from Christianity, or at best pays lip service to them, can justly claim to be an educational activity or avoid the charge of indoctrination.

Third, it is by no means clear that there is such a thing as a single 'Christian heritage'. From the time of the early church, as reflected in the New Testament documents themselves, Christianity has always been a diverse phenomenon, reflecting a wide range of traditions, doctrines and beliefs. It is not clear which Christian tradition should be offered, which set of Christian values brought into the classroom. Apart from the fundamental problem of distinguishing between Catholic, Protestant and Orthodox forms of Christianity, together with the wealth of plurality within each sub-division, we are also faced with distinctions between conservative, liberal, charismatic and various radical versions of the Christian story. Does the Christian heritage, for example, include those Anglican priests who do not believe in the existence of God?

Fourth, the rhetoric of 'the return to Christian values' fails to distinguish between Christian culture and Christian belief. To accept 'Christian' values, to uphold the ethics of the ten commandments and the sermon on the mount, cannot be equated with the specific commitment to Christian truth claims regarding the existence and nature of God and His interaction with His creation. 'Christendom' and 'Christianity' are not necessarily one and the same thing.

Behind all these objections stands an even more fundamental issue, one that raises the question of the nature of education itself. On the one hand, education may be seen as being concerned with the autonomous growth of individuals, capable of thinking for themselves, of taking responsibility for their behaviour. On the other hand, education may be seen as being concerned with ethical and social reform, with the inculcation in pupils of a sense of morality. Peter Gay (1987), in his monumental survey of the thought of the Enlightenment has seen in the tension between these two approaches a 'dilemma of heroic proportions': how do teachers balance the desire for reform with the desire to promote individual freedom? He suggests that for the majority, the solution has been to place the need for reform above that of autonomy. However, this has led educators through

> the devious and embarrassing detours of repression and manipulation that were a denial or mockery of the world they hoped to bring into being: the very methods used to distribute the fruits of enlightenment seemed calculated to frustrate enlightenment itself (p.497).

It is a relatively simple task to apply Gay's argument to current demands for a return to confessionalism. Such demands place the desire for a return to traditional 'Christian' values above a desire for the autonomous development of individual pupils and the growth of their ability to, in the words of Kant, one of the key philosophers of the Enlightenment, 'have the courage to think for themselves'. By presenting religion in a confessional form that does not reflect its actual nature and place in society, religious education allows itself to become a tool in a process of social engineering.

The road to a renewed confessionalism can only be taken if we choose to 'pre-package' a notion of what exactly constitutes our Christian heritage. Such 'pre-packaging' will necessarily involve the bypassing of the ambiguity of secularism, pluralism, the relationship between Christianity and culture, and the diversity of Christianity itself. Such a process will deny pupils the right to appropriate these issues for themselves, deny them the opportunity of an education in the complex reality and ambiguity of contemporary religion. Instead, it offers an education within extremely paternalistic boundaries, one which our pupils will all too easily see through and recognize for what it is, one that can only lead to an increase in religious illiteracy.

A resurgent liberalism?

To question the programme of liberal religious education immediately makes one vulnerable to misunderstanding, since for many the only alternative to the openness, freedom, tolerance and respect for individuals associated with the phrase 'liberalism' is some form of narrow-minded, blinkered imposition of ideas that ignores any alternative position. The latter is not on my agenda. On the contrary, my concern is to try to 'out-liberal' liberalism, to find ways of offering pupils greater freedom and openness, to draw out the necessary link between tolerance and honesty. There are ways in which 'liberalism' has itself become closed and narrow-minded, ways in which it has, like confessionalism before it, forced religious traditions into a paternalistic framework in which they do not belong.

The liberal framework

To understand the current consensus we need to step back for a while and make the effort to explore its historical origins. Liberalism, in the sense in which I am using the term, has its roots in the Enlightenment, that cultural and intellectual revolution that 300 years ago gave birth to our modern western civilization. At its heart lay the development of modern science: the work of Newton, Gallileo and others offered a new set of 'facts' about the world that both appeared to challenge the Christian tradition and at the same time seemed to offer clarity, coherence, certainty and objectivity in its results.

These scientific certainties seemed far more attractive than many of the now rather dubious beliefs associated with religion. As any child knows, we need no more than an apple to demonstrate publicly the reality of gravity, but is is a little harder to prove key aspects of religious belief: the existence of God for example, or the truth of the Christian doctrine of incarnation.

Thus the Enlightenment came to distinguish between 'knowledge' and 'belief'. The 'knowledge' provided by science was seen as an objective, certain and public affair, something no one in their right mind would dream of questioning (unless of course they belong to the 'Flat Earth Society'!). The 'beliefs' associated with religion were, on the other hand, seen as subjective, uncertain and essentially private affairs. While acceptance of scientific knowledge came to be seen as in some sense obligatory, acceptance of religious belief became an optional extra.

The problem for the Enlightenment was how to develop a society that accepted both 'knowledge' and 'belief' as part and parcel of its cultural heritage. Here liberalism comes in: human beings must be seen as essentially free and should never be coerced into accepting a 'belief' on any grounds other than their own free choice. This doctrine of freedom of belief could potentially be a recipe for conflict and dispute between different belief systems, so a second key principle was introduced by liberalism. Alongside freedom of belief was placed the requirement that believers tolerated the beliefs of others. As long as you kept your belief a private affair you were free to believe whatever you like, but as soon as you attempted to impose your belief on others you proved yourself to be intolerant of others, and hence to have strayed outside the liberal framework.

It is on these twin pillars, of freedom of belief and tolerance of the beliefs of others, that the liberal vision of a flourishing, integrated multicultural society is based, and it was to schools that liberals turned as one of the key agents that could provide the liberal cement of society. The liberal model sees religious education as a process of informing children about the plural belief systems operating in our multicultural society and of nurturing their acceptance and tolerance of the richness of this diversity.

There seems to be no doubt whatsoever that western liberalism has had great success in moving towards this vision of tolerance and acceptance in diversity. We no longer burn at the stake those who believe differently to ourselves; we question the justice of armed conflict in the name of religion; we have anti-racist legislation on our statute books to give teeth to the notion of tolerance; we have equal opportunities policies in schools that act as a watchdog to guard against any form of inequality rooted in race, class, gender or sexual orientation. In questioning the liberal framework I do not wish to deny its success, nor to question its fundamental importance and value, but rather to build on it for the future. But, I suggest, the future lies in the acknowledgement of serious flaws in the fabric of liberalism. If these flaws are allowed to continue unnoticed then the ideals of liberalism will remain grounded in foundations of sand.

Flaws in the liberal framework

In order to shed light on some of the flaws in liberalism, let us take as an example probably the most powerful world view, alongside that of western liberalism, in the world today: Islam. Indeed, recent international events in the Gulf have suggested that, with the collapse of communism, the relationship between Islam and the liberal west is, alongside issues of militarism, ecology and the third world, one of the key issues facing the future of humanity. The western bloc has shown itself as being not above the need to scapegoat non-western powers as a means of asserting its own identity and deflecting attention from its own failings. We may no longer have the 'evil empire', to quote a past President of the United States of America, in the form of the USSR to stand up to, but is it too cynical to suggest that Muslim countries, particularly in the oil-rich middle east, provide a suitable alternative?

Islam is not a 'liberal' religion. By that I do not mean that Muslims lack tolerance, compassion, a desire for peaceful co-existence and mutual understanding, despite the fact that some of the rhetoric spouted by the western media and politicians may ask us to believe otherwise. (There is a constant danger of selecting out the activities of certain movements associated with Islam and using them to stereotype their outlook as a norm all Muslims adhere to. One might just as easily identify the activities of the South African security forces as 'Christian'). No, what I do mean is that the heart of Islam lies not in the liberal distinction between knowledge and belief, but in submission to the will of Allah as it is revealed in the Qur'an. Muslim tolerance is rooted in that revelation, not in the tolerance of western liberalism.

Liberalism is a product of the west. Perhaps uniquely in western education we as teachers of religious education are asked to deal with non-western world views in the classroom. Apart from some aspects of liberal Christianity and Judaism, it is true to say that all religious systems have their roots in non-liberal, and in many cases, non-western, cultural systems. Again, let me stress, this does not mean that these religions have no concern with human understanding and tolerance: could anyone seriously say that of the teachings of, say, Hinduism and Buddhism? Yet the concern for the tolerant development of our common humanity that lies close to the heart of Hinduism and Buddhism comes from those world views themselves, from the Hindu and Buddhist beliefs about the nature of reality. They most certainly did not learn these values from the liberal west, though they may well have encountered western colonialism and imperialism. Yet in the current consensus of religious education we force these non-liberal religious traditions into our own western liberal framework.

Women and The Satanic Verses

Let me plunge into the deep end and offer two concrete examples as a way of putting flesh on these bones: Islamic reaction to the publication of *The Satanic Verses,* and to the liberal western attitude towards the issue of gender.

First, *The Satanic Verses.* When Salman Rushdie wrote and then published his book, he was an ex-Muslim guilty in the eyes of the Islamic community of blasphemy towards Allah, on the basis of Allah's revelation to humankind in the pages of the Qur'an. The reaction of the world-wide Muslim community was varied, though the imposition of the *fatwa* in the form of the death sentence, was by no means universally supported by Muslims, despite the impression given by sections of the British press.

For liberal westerners the controversy posed a dilemma of epic proportions. The liberal concept of freedom of belief, and of expression of that belief, lead quite naturally to support for Mr Rushdie, and indeed the positive and vocal support of the western literary community seems to have been reflected in popular opinion. But what of the liberal demand for tolerance? The liberal multiculturalism adopted in British schools, calling for mutual toleration and acceptance, seemed to have hit a brick wall: here was a belief that, from a western perspective apparently, could not be tolerated, yet it lay at the very heart of the world view of the largest and most influential ethnic minority group in the country. The reality seemed to be that western liberalism, in calling for toleration, was essentially paternalistic: we can tolerate your belief system, provided you keep within the framework of our liberalism. You are free to adhere to the beliefs of Islam, provided you keep those beliefs a private affair, and do not allow them to overflow into any form of public or political action. Yet for Islam there is no, and can never be any, distinction between the private and public spheres; that notion is a creation of liberalism itself.

If I believe that freedom of expression and the right of Salman Rushdie to write and publish whatever he wishes are of fundamental value, I can do so only by acknowledging the tension between this position and the position of Islam. To assume that my view is correct, and that somehow Islam is lacking or inadequate in its approach, and consequently is in need of a little openness and liberalization, could only be an act of patronization that failed to appreciate the true nature of Islamic belief. To accept the tension, and respect the autonomy and freedom of Islam, whilst rejecting its conclusions, in some sense may be said to 'out-liberal' liberalism.

Second, women in Islam. I was once privileged to tutor a group of Muslim students studying at a university institute of education. Both the institute itself and the students union had what seemed to me to be well thought-out and effectively operating equal opportunities policies, policies which I was happy to give assent to.

A few weeks into term a number of the Muslim students, all perhaps significantly enough women, approached me with a dilemma concerning this policy. To put it in their own words, 'this equal opportunities policy seems to us essentially racist'. They found themselves faced with a system that promised to tolerate their religious beliefs, culture and ethnic background, but not if that were to include acceptance of a Muslim understanding of the role of women in society. They were living daily with an attitude directed towards them by some fellow students that suggested that their culture was in some way inadequate, that they themselves needed liberating from the claustrophobic structures Islamic society imposed upon them. They explained to me how their place in Islamic society gave them a freedom to assert their existence as women without the pressures that the 'freedom' western women had achieved this century had to cope with.

I do not wish to get involved with the pros and cons of this particular argument here. It is sufficient to point out that the Muslim position is rooted in an understanding of reality significantly at variance from that of western liberalism, and that the reality, whether or not one agrees with the particular argument, was that the Muslim students found the liberal rhetoric of tolerance to be a limited one. For them liberal tolerance was qualified, again, in a paternalistic way: we will tolerate your Muslim faith, provided you keep it within the limits of our own liberalism. You are free to believe anything you like about the place of women in society, provided you also allow women in your community the 'freedom' that western women have gained for themselves through their struggle for emancipation.

Though my own belief may be that the feminist movement in the west is one of fundamental importance and value in our developing understanding of the nature of humanity, I learnt from my Muslim students that I could hold that belief only *in tension* with alternative understandings of this issue. My only alternative to living with this tension and acknowledging the reality of the dispute is to patronize my Muslim students, and that I was not willing to do, out of respect for their freedom and autonomy. In this situation, an acceptance of tension and conflict and a refusal to patronize, marks, I would argue, a move forward in the debate which actually 'out-liberals' the prevailing liberal orthodoxy.

In other words, there is a sense in which liberalism has itself become a 'closed' system, able to work happily within its own framework but uncertain as to how to treat those cultures that are not a part of it. By imposing its own standards on those non-liberal systems it becomes patronizing, and hence contradicts its own demand for open tolerance. My suggestion is that the way for liberalism to move forward is not to reject its own standards and values, but to recognize and become conscious of the reality that non-liberal cultures do actually exist in Britain. The implication of this is that somehow society needs to begin to accept the reality of unresolved tensions within its plural diversity, tensions that are unlikely to disappear overnight and wnich liberalism is not capable of papering over. The question society must then face is that of how it can live with, and develop creatively within, these tensions.

Implications for religious education

If, in religious education, we are taking seriously the plurality of world faiths, then we must beware the danger of imposing on those faiths a liberal framework. There is a danger of western liberalism slipping into a form of post-colonial paternalism. This is, I believe, a trap that liberal religious education has inadvertently fallen into. Let me give two examples.

First, liberal religious education has, I would argue, perpetuated a *myth of the nature of religion*. In seeking to avoid the pitfalls of confessionalism, it has attempted to offer a neutral description of the world's key faiths. All religions could be objectively described in terms of a series of common 'dimensions', most popularly seen in terms of their doctrines, myths, ethics, rituals, religious experiences and social structures. Thus for example, we could ask pupils to look, under the heading of 'doctrine', at 'sacred books' or 'founders of the faith', or under the heading of 'ritual', at 'places of worship' or 'rites of passage'. This would give the clear impression that the cultural phenomena of religion were all variations on a single entity, 'religion'. Thus, for example 'founders of the faith' would equate Abraham in Judaism, Jesus in Christianity, and Muhammed in Islam as having similar functions, that of starting off a particular religious tradition. In terms of a secular cultural history this may well be true. However, the reality is that, seen in terms of theological perspectives of the different faith communities, Abraham, Jesus and Muhammed have very different roles to play in their respective traditions, and to view them all as 'founders' does justice to none of them. For Jews, Jesus was a false Messiah, for Christians the incarnation of God, for Muslims a prophet: not only are these self-contradictory beliefs, since Jesus cannot by definition be all of these at once, but also in none of them is Jesus correctly seen as being primarily a 'founder' of a faith. This myth that the variety of world faiths have a common nature and structure fails to do justice to the faiths involved, which in almost every case see themselves as being distinctive and unique entities.

Second, liberal religious education has also perpetuated the *myth of the equality of religions*. Indeed this was something that the liberal model openly advocated and fought for. All religions are to be treated equally, in a neutral and tolerant manner. Fair enough, one might well say; however, the consequences of this process need to be noted. The demand for neutrality meant that the truth claims of individual religions were seen as private issues that were not to be dealt with in the classroom, ignoring the reality that at the heart of each of the religions being dealt with lies a claim to the possession of the unique and ultimate truth about reality. Thus, in the classroom the demand for openness and neutrality became in reality a claim that each, in its own way, offers an equally valid path to truth. Yet this is precisely what the world's faiths, in their own self-understanding as opposed to the liberal interpretation, do not claim.

Both these myths are the result of the application of a liberal framework to non-liberal world views. Their adoption was the result of a desire to utilize religious traditions to support and develop a liberal multicultural society, and as such reflect not the self-understanding of the adherents of those traditions themselves, but rather their accommodation by western scholars and teachers to their own liberal framework. Liberal religious education thus in reality actually entails a paternalistic 'westernization' of the world's faiths.

As with our discussion of confessionalism, we are drawn to the conclusion that the liberal road that many involved in religious education have embarked upon is in reality a dead end. Despite its rhetoric of freedom and openness, liberal religious education acts in a paternalistic manner, imposing on religion a set of myths that are concerned not with the development of any intelligent and informed understanding of the complex nature of religion, but with utilizing the subject to support a particular programme of social reform and development. It involves a paternalistic pre-packaging of various religious traditions in a form that avoids their ambiguities, contradictions and diversity. If liberalism cannot do justice to these traditions then it would appear that we are dealing with a benign form of social engineering, rather than with genuine education. Indeed, it is possible to hear used with increasing frequency in religious education circles the telling phrase, 'indoctrination into a liberal world view'.

Beyond educational paternalism

If contemporary religious education is asked to decide between choosing the path of a renewed confessionalism or a resurgent liberalism, then I would suggest that its choice is between two dead ends. Both involve a similar process, despite the very different forms of religious education they advocate: a process of educational paternalism.

In essence both see the ambiguity of religion in the context of a pluralistic and increasingly secular society as an issue to be avoided. Both set out to gloss over this ambiguity by reaching a solution *before* the process of education begins. The role that the religious educator is asked to adopt is to pre-package religion into something acceptable to society, and then to inculcate the results of this pre-packaging in the minds of pupils. The result is that the next generation of pupils will be introduced to a religious ideology, whether it be a confessional Christian one or a liberal humanistic one, without the freedom to explore and come to any understanding of alternative perspectives.

Furthermore, the issue of which ideology will prevail will be worked out at the level of political infighting between conservatives and liberals. The focus of *this* debate is on the issue of competing visions about the future development of society and the conflicting values of those who hold contrasting blueprints as to what that society should be like. Both have in common the belief that religious education is not an end in itself, but essentially a tool for a process of social engineering directed towards a morally and spiritually rejuvenated society.

This seems to me to be an unacceptable choice: if we are genuinely concerned about religious education and the religious understanding of the next generation, then it seems to me that a third road needs to be explored, one that goes beyond the limitations of the current sterile debate between liberals and confessionalists.

Democracy and ultimate truth

In his book *A Theology of Auschwitz* Ulrich Simon (1978) attempts to do what to many seems impossible — to speak of a God of love in the face of the horrors of the holocaust:

> We are dealing with the deaths of millions, mostly non-combatant Jews, who had been rounded up and sent to various concentration-camps designed entirely for their extermination ... Auschwitz belongs to the past, thank God. But its multi-dimensional range of evil extends to the present and throws its shadow over the future. It is ... the comprehensive and realistic symbol of the greatest possible evil which still threatens mankind (pp.11ff).

Events in the former Yugoslavia underline the prophetic nature of Simon's words: renewed armed conflict in the heart of civilized Europe, conflict that, if United Nations reports are correct, has reached the depth of the systemic rape of thousands of Muslim women as part of the process of 'ethnic cleansing'.

We do not need to look too far to discover other symptoms of the sickness of western democracy: rioting in inner-city areas, racial tension, a widening division between rich and poor, child abuse, the exploitation of the third world and the environment, the rising crime rate and lack of respect for individuals — the list seems endless. Little seems to have changed: the agenda of the need for a moral and spiritual rejuvenation in society seems as important now as it was in 1944.

The problem with the programmes for moral and spiritual rejuvenation offered by confessionalism and liberalism respectively is their lack of insight into the depth and complexity of the problem, and hence also the simplistic nature of their proposed solutions. Both at heart seem more utopian than realistic. Can a 'return to traditional values' or the demand for 'tolerance and freedom' really respond to the depth of the evil and meaninglessness of our current moral vacuum? Are not both guilty of 'ill-fated optimism, which would spirit away evil, sickness, and death by pretending that they are not there' (Simon, 1978, p.21).

Much derision was aimed at the Secretary of State for Education, John Patten, when he spoke of the need to bring a sense of heaven and hell back into the classroom. However, might it be just possible that it was of this issue, of the need to take with the utmost seriousness right and wrong, good and evil, heaven and hell, rather than sweep the inhumanity of man towards fellow man under the carpet, that he was actually speaking?

Reason, autonomy and education

If we are to take seriously the place of religious education in supporting the future moral and spiritual recovery of society, then we need above all to recover a sense of hard-nosed realism. We need to move away from an innocent optimism that has nothing to say to us in the face of the realities of abused children and the killing fields of Cambodia. But how might this be achieved? If we want our children to take responsibility for their own morality, and the morality of the next generation, then imposing a used, disputed and, some would even argue, discredited 'confessional' or 'liberal' blueprint is surely unlikely to equip them to avoid the mistakes of their parents and grandparents.

Such a benign paternalistic approach to schooling needs to be replaced with one that respects the autonomy and reason of individuals: that allows them to come face-to-face with personal and social dilemmas in a manner in which they can make sense of them in intelligent and informed ways; in a manner in which they can appropriate for themselves the complexities of the issues involved; in a manner in which they can seek, in a democratic context, solutions for their generation. If we are going to take education for citizenship seriously, then we must accept that citizenship entails freedom to play a full part in the democratic process in a way in which wisdom and insight may take precedence over propaganda and image.

To return again to Professor Simon:

The dangers which threaten our society arise out of ills which lie in the past. They have remained uncured, and it is in the interest of civilised normality *to lay bare the secrets* of those ills so that they may be rendered less menacing (1978, p.13, emphasis added).

'To lay bare the secrets': the role of education, and hence the new agenda for religious education, needs to be rooted in the rejection of simple solutions to complex moral issues, and the acceptance of the role of education in offering pupils the skills and insights with which to understand and interpret the complex and ambiguous world we live in.

Ultimate meaning

What role has religious education in this new educational agenda? The philosopher and educationalist John Dewey, in his classic *Democracy and Education* (1966) suggests that:

To say that education is a social function, securing direction and development in the immature through their participation in the life of the group to which they belong, is to say in effect that education will vary with the quality of life which prevails in a group (p.81).

What 'quality of life' should education for democratic citizenship be rooted in? If the democratic process is one of ongoing change and development led by the individual autonomous votes of each citizen, then surely we need to look to a quality that enables young citizens to take on this responsibility in an informed way. This must involve taking on board the complexities of a modern pluralistic society, to learn to move forward within its tensions rather than whitewashing over them.

The theologian Paul Tillich saw a link between religion and that which is of 'ultimate concern' for humanity. What, amidst the pace and demands of life in the modern west is of ultimate interest, ultimate value, ultimate importance? The answers, of course, will depend on how we see the ultimate nature of our universe and humanity's place within it. This seems to me to be a crucial point. Morality does not exist in a vacuum: there is a direct link between the way the reality of our universe and our place within it are understood, and the morality we in fact adopt.

If, as the atheistic humanism claims, there is no meaning and truth transcending space and time, then our morality and ultimate values will probably develop in the form of some kind of pragmatic humanism: make the best of life before you die, be honest with yourself and try not to hurt others, or some similar formula. If, on the other hand, we accept the claims of religious traditions that ultimate truth and meaning have their roots in some form of transcendence, whether it be in the nature of God or some other transcendent reality, then ultimate truth and meaning will take on a very different set of values. Christians, for example, will come to see ultimate value in terms of their relationship with God in the framework provided by the Christian scheme of fall, justification and atonement, and will see their lives in terms of the Christian story of creation, incarnation and final judgement.

Tillich's focus on ultimate concern is thus not enough. Our ultimate concern may be a limited one, one that puts our humanity into an inadequate strait-jacket, hampering growth towards a discovery of our true humanity. If, for example, my ultimate concern is whether Tottenham Hotspur will ever win the Premier League Championship in my life time, my humanity immediately becomes limited: not because of the (sadly) futile nature of the hope, but because there are actually far more important things in life than football, if only I can throw off the blinkers of my fanaticism and learn to see them. Such fanaticism is, in religious language, idolatry. Our ultimate concern, our ultimate values, morality and belief, can thus be misplaced ones. Thus ultimate concern needs to be linked with the question of ultimate truth: are the things that I am ultimately concerned about in harmony with the way reality ultimately is? Or am I living a life grounded in a false illusion? The question of value cannot be torn apart from the question of truth.

This then, I would suggest, is what should be at the heart of a new agenda for religious education: to educate future citizens in a democracy by refusing to give patronizing and simplistic answers to questions that are of central importance. To enable our pupils to reach a depth of understanding of the moral and social dilemmas before humanity we must allow them to see what these dilemmas and questions look like in the light of the question of ultimate truth. 'Liberalism' and 'confessionalism', by pre-packaging religious answers rather than addressing religious questions are involved not in education but in social engineering. They offer pupils pre-packaged value systems that have at their heart specific answers to the question of what actually constitutes ultimate truth.

In the light of the ultimate evil of the Shoah, itself the product, in part at least, of social engineering, our society and our children deserve better than to be forced to feed only on the scraps that fall from the squabbling between 'liberals' and 'confessionalists'. If we are to take democracy seriously, then we must replace indoctrination and social engineering with a realistic education. We must be willing to put our trust in our pupils' ability to appropriate the challenges facing humanity for themselves in a form of religious education whose agenda looks beyond liberalism and confessionalism.

CHAPTER 4
Religious Ambiguity and Truth

Religious literacy

We suggested in the previous chapter that the programmes of confessionalism and liberalism contain fundamental flaws that would appear to demand that religious education looks elsewhere for a new agenda as it attempts to move forward in the wake of the 1988 Education Act. Is there, then, the possibility of a new framework for the subject, of an approach that goes beyond confessionalism and liberalism? The current state of play in religious education would appear to ignore three crucial issues: the truth of religion; the ambiguity of religion in modern society; and the possibility of a religious literacy not confined to the limitations of a paternalistic education system. What might religious education look like if each of these is placed on the agenda and taken seriously?

In adopting the phrases 'religious literacy' and 'religious illiteracy', I am using a little poetic licence: they are used here to refer respectively to the ability, and inability, to reflect, communicate and act in an informed, intelligent and sensitive manner towards the phenomenon of religion. Our society could be said to be a profoundly religiously illiterate one, and this constitutes a state of affairs that demands closer inspection by anyone concerned with the development of religious education.

'Human kind cannot bear very much reality': these words of T. S. Elliot (1974, p.190) were directed, at least in part, towards the spiritual and cultural void he believed lay at the heart of modern western society — a society that prefers the cheap option of hiding behind the propaganda, stereotypes and slogans of politicians, the media and advertisers, rather than the costly option of facing up squarely and honestly to the complex dilemmas that lie before it. The former choice offers an oasis of security and stability amidst the tensions and pressures of the modern world, the latter places a question mark over the assumptions on which we base our lives. All too often we choose the former, trusting the slogans and not asking if their foundations are of rock or sand.

This situation encompasses contemporary approaches to religion. There seems to be a poverty at the heart of the language we use to explore and make sense of religious questions. Those with the courage to question the barriers created by this situation soon become objects of ridicule and contempt. Take, as a classic example, the 'Durham Affair': the reaction of the media to the Bishop of Durham's suggestion that at the resurrection God was not merely performing a 'conjuring trick with bones'.

Whatever our personal opinions on the bishop's views, it is important to be aware of his motivation in asking the questions he did. If one follows through the debate carefully it soon becomes clear that his concern was to challenge a form of religious sloganizing that reduced the profundity of the Christian doctrine of the resurrection of Christ (whether or not it is true is at this stage irrelevant), to an event that would be at home on the 'Paul Daniel's Magic Show'. For David Jenkins the issue seems to be the fundamental one of the possibility of religious literacy.

The reaction of the media to this attempt to raise the level of public debate was sad, though predictable, as slogan was heaped upon slogan in the attack on him. We were told not only that the bishop of Durham does not believe in the resurrection, itself an open question dependent on what exactly the phrase 'resurrection' means, but also that this editorial viewpoint had been confirmed by the Almighty himself, who apparently chose to express his displeasure at the renegade bishop by causing a bolt of lightning to descend from the heavens and strike York Minster.

One of the key causes of this poverty in religious debate would appear to be rooted in its rupture from the intellectual traditions that offer the opportunity to put such conversations on a higher plain. The popular press, with a few noble exceptions, seems all too willing to give column space to the type of religious blockbuster that offers us the 'truth about Jesus the Church does not want us to know', or sets out to reveal how the Dead Sea Scrolls 'undermine the very foundations of Christian faith'. Almost without exception such publications are written in complete ignorance of the basic, painstaking and at times even rather ponderous and unexciting, scholarship that is the bread and butter of research in university theological departments throughout the world. They are the type of book that no serious academic publishing house would touch with a bargepole, and which offer arguments that any undergraduate theology student could refute with ease.

Thus the privatization of religious belief in the liberal west, coupled with the notion of freedom of belief, seems to have given birth to an anarchic pseudo-scholarship that is happy to ignore the demands of academic integrity. This situation can also be observed in the particularly western phenomena of the growth of what are labelled 'new religious movements'. At their worst these constitute a 'do-it-yourself' approach to religious belief. Individuals and groups, against a background of a vague impressionistic fascination with the occult, mysticism and the so-called 'new-age' movement, simply sit down and produce a new religion from scratch. The most obvious current example of this phenomenon is to be found in David Ike's claim to be the Son of God, though a visit to Glastonbury or California will reveal countless others. Sociologically this seem to be an extension of the search for alternative life-styles outside of the 'system' that flourished in the 1960s. The phenomenon, though, is not just confined to such esoteric cults: it is commonplace to hear individuals offer their own constructions of reality, and with a little probing discover that they have taken little time to research their statements in any depth.

This poverty of religious dialogue, rooted in the rupture from intellectual and cultural roots and producing 'DIY religion', would seem to lead us inevitably to the reality of religious 'fundamentalism'. This word can easily be abused if applied to all those who take religious belief seriously, particularly if the belief is at odds with western liberalism. It does, however, have a viable currency if applied to those religious groups who use their retreat to commitment as a means of closing out religious conversation by building protective walls within which the 'saved' find security, and through which no voice of dialogue can be heard. It is in fundamentalism of this type that we encounter the heart of religious illiteracy. Such illiteracy offers the comfort and safety of the simple clear-cut answer. Here atheist and religious believer alike (since fundamentalism is not uniquely a religious phenomenon), motivated either by deep commitment or apathy, adopt the process of withdrawing from open debate, defining *their* particular version of the 'truth', and setting up barriers that will protect this truth from awkward questions.

It is hard to resist the conclusion from all this that somewhere along the line the religious questions became too complex and challenging for modern society, which opted to resort to the security of empty slogans, producing in the process our current religiously illiterate culture.

Contemporary religious education must, it seems to me, shoulder its portion of the guilt in having in some small way helped create and reinforce this state of affairs. Knowing that religion is, and has always been, a subject of heated controversy and deep-rooted ambiguity, religious educators chose to ignore this fact. A religious education that pre-packages its product, offering students only one point of access to religion, one single interpretive framework, will inevitably descend into mere sloganism, however sophisticated and articulate such slogans appear to be.

Religious education surely has a moral duty and responsibility to challenge this descent into religious illiteracy. If education is about insight, knowledge and wisdom then religious educators must be held accountable for their role in enhancing or hindering the process of producing a religiously literate society. What religious education desperately needs is a way of proceeding that allows students access to the complexities of religious belief, one that avoids the simple solutions, one that can take the pupil beyond the slogans and rhetoric pumped out to them day after day. The way forward, I suggest, is to welcome and embrace the question of religious truth.

The truth of religion

It is, of course, unfashionable in the extreme to suggest that religious education should be primarily concerned with the question of religious truth. Indeed, the history of the subject between 1944 and 1988 can be read as an account of the closure of the issue of truth. Even if we accept that confessionalism was primarily concerned with Christian truth, and not with the utilization of Christian virtue for non-Christian ends, certainly with the advent of the liberal paradigm the question of truth had been removed firmly from the agenda.

The immediate cause of this was the need to avoid the charge of indoctrination and to observe a methodological neutrality. This was linked with a concern with the positive function of religion as a force for change in society rather than with an interest in religion for religion's sake. If we observe a strict neutrality because of our search for religious tolerance, then the conflicting nature of truth claims must be taken off the agenda. The deeper cause is to be found in the privatization of belief, the withdrawal of religious truth claims from the public sphere. If truth is essentially subjective and arbitrary, then its exploration cannot be part of any public educational agenda. In the USA this argument has been embodied in legislation that removes religious education from the curriculum of public schools in the name of freedom of belief.

There is a profound irony at the heart of this situation. On the one hand religious education systematically ignores questions of religious truth, yet on the other there is not a religious belief system in existence that does not have the issue of ultimate truth at the very core of its being.

The ontological question

At the heart of religion's concern with ultimate truth stands the 'ontological' question: 'How does it come about that the universe exists?'; 'Why is there something rather than nothing?'; 'Is there anything beyond space and time?'.

Imagine you had access to a time machine that could take you back in time to the point beyond the beginnings of the time-space continuum, to that 'nothingness' before which, or within which, or out of which (our normal language here appears so inadequate) the 'big bang' occurred. What might you find? God? Nothing? If God, then where did God come from? If nothing, then where did the 'big bang' come from? At the heart of this question is rooted the question of ultimate truth, the problem of the fundamental meaning and purpose of our universe, and hence of humanity and our own individual, transient, solitary lives.

We seem to have two basic choices. The first is the way of *transcendence:* beyond space and time stands a reality, a being, a God, or gods, that created and gives ultimate meaning to our universe. Such a reality constitutes a fixed point, beyond which explanation need not go. God, in the western theistic tradition, is self-creating. To ask the question 'Where did God come from?' is to misunderstand the meaning of the term. 'God' simply *is*, the ultimate explanation of questions of meaning and truth is found here. Ultimate meaning and truth are thus rooted in a reality that transcends the limits of our universe and its space and time.

The second possibility points us towards *immanence:* our universe is simply all that there is. A Year 7 pupil grappling with this issue in the context of her imaginary journey into the origins of space and time once offered me a clear insight into this possibility. She arrived at the 'nothingness' before the 'big bang' and left her time-machine. Unable to see anything she lit a match, but this was of no help. Frustrated, she threw it away: it landed on the fuel tank of the vehicle. 'Bang!': the universe had begun. The universe, reality, is self-creating and is quite simply all that there *is*. To look to some transcendent beyond is a dead end: truth and meaning are to be found entirely within the universe itself; are rooted in our immanent world.

Transcendence or immanence? The ontological question seems to offer us a fundamental and crucial choice. It is a choice that opens up the question of truth. Not the truth which I have come to accept for myself, since what is true for me may not be what is true about reality. No, the objective truth remains reality regardless of what I, or the rest of humanity choose to accept. Our moral freedom to accept the truth we choose does not guarantee that our choice will be correct. It is quite possible that we have chosen falsely, and that the reality we accept is in fact an illusion. We may rightly claim freedom from being coerced into the beliefs of others through bad education or indoctrination, but we can only claim freedom to believe what we like in the face of what is genuinely true at the expense of a journey into falsehood and illusion.

Transcendence, immanence and nihilism

The choice between transcendence or immanence is but the start of humanity's religious and secular quest for understanding and meaning, is but the beginning of our all too human attempts to align ourselves with, to get in tune with, the ultimate truth of our universe, our environment, our society and ourselves.

The way of transcendence leads us into a maze of conflicting possibilities and brings us face-to-face with the reality of religious pluralism. This religious quest offers no simple solutions, yet it stands at the heart of just about every human culture with the exception of that of the modern western world.

Our exploration leads us to religious systems that have died out; to the religions of the ancient Egyptians, Greeks and Aztecs, It leads us to primal religion, those religious systems that continue to flourish in societies relatively untouched by the spread of 'enlightened' western culture. It leads us to the east, to Buddhism, Hinduism and Sikhism. It leads us to the west: to the monotheistic tradition rooted in the myths and legends of the Hebrew patriarchs; to the battles between the followers of YHWH and Canaanite fertility religions; to the Jewish prophets and scholars; to the life of Jesus of Nazareth and the birth of Christianity; to Muhammed, Gabriel and the Qur'an. The ontological question forces upon us the issue of transcendent truth, in the process throwing us head-first into the complexity and diversity of the religious quest of humanity. But might this quest be a futile one? Might not the ultimate truth be rooted in our immanent world alone?

Newtonian science used mathematics to measure space and to measure time. Yet a sequence of numbers can travel on into infinity: start counting upwards 1, 2, 3 — and there is no need ever to stop. Did this not make space and time infinite? Did it not suggest that time and space travel on into infinity: that there is no beginning or end to time, nor a brick wall at the end of the universe? Yet was this notion of infinity not something we used to attribute to God? Has not the universe taken on the attributes of God Himself (the possibility of describing God as 'she' did not exist during the Enlightenment)? Is not the implication of this that transcendence may be replaced with immanence, that it is the universe not God which is the entity that 'explains itself'?

Thus the Enlightenment came to place a question mark over the previous assumption that truth and meaning must be rooted in transcendence. Link this up with the scepticism with which religious traditions, authority and doctrines were now to be approached, and we come face-to-face with the possibilities of secularism, agnosticism and atheism.

If the truth lies here, in a purely immanent world, then what sense are we to make of transcendent religious beliefs? The philosopher Feuerbach came up with a simple and highly influential answer. He simply turned the first creation myth in the book of Genesis on its head: 'Then humanity itself said, "Let us make a God in our image, after our likeness"'. Belief in God and notions of transcendence are thus creations of the human imagination, of humanity's desire to transcend itself. Theology becomes anthropology.

Religious belief thus becomes the ultimate illusion: one which according to Nietzsche justified human beings in holding fast to their inadequacy and weakness; one which according to Marx gave comfort to the victims of capitalism and legitimated the actions of its victors; one which according to Freud offered the human unconscious the security of a father who transcended the limitations of human parents.

It was but a short step to logical positivism — a philosophy that, though now discredited, has filtered down in contemporary society. A statement is true when we can show how we can verify it through our senses: an apple falls on our head, so the language of gravity is verified as true. A statement is meaningless if is not capable of verification: I cannot show through my senses that God exists, therefore language of God is simply meaningless. Reality and ultimate truth are one and the same as the brute physical fact of our universe; all else is simply devoid of meaning, reality and truth.

How then do we live in a brute physical world in which meaning is limited to physical matter? Do we invoke the myth of Sisyphus: that figure in Greek mythology condemned in Hades to roll a rock to the top of a hill only to see it roll back down again, and forced to repeat the operation throughout eternity? Is there no ultimate meaning to life beyond our physical existence? Are all our actions fundamentally futile? Can we at least cling to the fact that unlike Sisyphus death will one day relieve us of this burden of futility?

Such nihilism remains present in the west, whether in the superficial popular culture of 'punk rock', or in the profound attempts to rediscover our humanity in the shadow of the gas chambers of Auschwitz. Western culture has not been ambivalent about this challenge to humanity. Against nihilism it has embraced a variety of forms of humanism: types of existentialism, Marxism, pragmatism, utilitarianism, etc. It has affirmed that there *is* meaning in an immanent, Godless universe, and further that this meaning may be positively embraced. It is a meaning to be discovered rooted in our humanity, in our wisdom and creativity, in the moral absolute contained in the demand that we treat each other as ends in ourselves, that we go about our lives treating others as we would like to be treated.

Transcendence or immanence? Both claim that ultimate truth is a reality in the face of a nihilism that denies any possibility of absolute meaning. We simply cannot escape from these issues, unless of course we choose ignorance and the fundamentalism of an unexamined life. Yet the issues cloud into contradiction: all cannot be true, most must be illusion. If we take the question of truth seriously we are forced to embrace the phenomenon of ambiguity.

The ambiguity of religion

Ambiguity, which stands at the heart of the ontological question itself, lies rooted in the plurality of possible truths offered by immanent and transcendent world views. This becomes clear as soon as we try to pull together a panoramic picture that can encompass the breadth of this pluralism.

One possible picture is that of *exclusivism:* belief systems are mutually incompatible entities. To profess adherence to one involves the rejection of all others. Truth and salvation are to be found only within the one, absolute truth claim of a particular religion; all the rest are false. Thus, to repeat an observation made in the previous chapter, the Jewish understanding of Jesus as a false Messiah is incompatible with the Christian doctrine of incarnation, which in turn is denied by Islamic belief in the prophethood of Jesus.

A second picture is that of *inclusivism:* ultimate truth is to be found only in one system, although others may contain elements of the truth. Thus, for example, Muslims see Jews and Christians as 'people of the book', and as such they do indeed have some knowledge of Allah, and this knowledge might eventually led them to a true submission to God. However, Islam stands above and beyond both religions as the culmination of Allah's revelation of His will towards humankind.

A third possibility that may be sketched out is that of *pluralism:* all religions contain aspects of ultimate truth and as such all offer legitimate paths for humanity to follow. The liberal version of this story has been particularly influential in contemporary religious education. All religions have common roots in an identical experience of the transcendence or divine. However, different cultural and historical traditions have meant that humanity has, at different times and in different places, come to express this experience in contrasting stories, teachings and doctrines. The truth claims of the world's religions are not thus true in themselves, but are rather true in so far as they give more or less adequate expression to the common underlying experience.

The question of the relationship between these contrasting pictures is a matter of ongoing debate. Once again, though, we must observe that it is a debate in which contemporary religious education does not take part. Rather, a single solution is drawn out and pre-packaged before the process of education itself begins. Confessionalism is committed to a benign form of exclusivism, while liberalism embraces with vigour the option of pluralism.

Faith and reason

The issue of the ambiguity of religion does not stop at the question of the relationship between different transcendent and immanent schemes. It also asks of us questions regarding the fundamental coherence and function of transcendent claims to truth. Can religious belief ever claim a reasonable, even rational foundation? A host of clear-cut answers have been offered to this question, yet when these are placed alongside one another no coherent pattern emerges.

For many it does not seem possible, in our age of enlightened reason, for religious belief to be seen as anything more than a superstitious remnant of a pre-scientific past. At best the phenomenon of religious belief can be studied from an anthropological viewpoint, telling us much about the way human beings operate, but nothing of a non-existent deity. At the other end of the spectrum stand those who would want to claim that we can indeed find a coherent foundation for religious belief, and that there is no need to embrace the accusation of superstition. Here once more we are faced with a number of options.

First, an acceptance of religious authority. At the heart of many religious systems is to be found the belief that our knowledge of God stems from God's action in revealing His or Her nature to the world, whether in historical events, sacred scripture or the teaching authority of a religious body. Within the logic of theology this would seem to make sense. If we accept that God is above and beyond us, omnipotent and omniscient, and that human inadequacy and fallibility can never properly comprehend His divinity, then the notion of divine revelation would seem to many to be a coherent one. The problem with the notion of revelation is a fundamental one though: how do we discern revelation? How do we distinguish between the plurality of claims to revelation? Are we not inevitably led back to some sort of authority, of sacred text or holy community? And how does such acceptance of authority avoid descending into fundamentalism?

Second, a foundation in experience. Descartes taught us to distrust authority and trust our own reason. If reason itself fails to bring us to knowledge of God, could we not at least trust our experience? Cannot we place human experience, imagination and artistic and moral insight above a dry abstract reason? Does not our sense of the beauty of the world, the wonder of creation, the spiritual experience contained within us allow us a glimpse of God that transcends reason and offers us deeper insight into the nature of reality? Cannot we learn to see religious culture and doctrine as an outward expression of this inner experience?

Third, a rehabilitated reason. We may accept that the old medieval arguments that sought to demonstrate the existence of God fail to achieve their task. However, is it not possible to construct a coherent picture of religious belief, rooted in experience and revelation, and drawing on contemporary ways of explaining the world, and out of all this construct a viable foundation for religious belief? Is such a process so different from the activities of scientists who draw together experience and the authority of the scientific community to construct the best possible picture of the way things actually are, on the basis of the knowledge and insight currently available?

Each of these positions, and many more, are the subject of a sustained and continuing debate, both within religious communities and the world of academia. Informed, intelligent people can be found defending any of them. It would seem arrogant, whichever position we personally adopt, to reject any others out of hand: to do so surely serves to open up the path to religious illiteracy.

Idealism and realism

Another key source of ambiguity is that of the relationship between an idealistic description of a belief system and the way it actually operates. Thus within any particular belief system we are likely to encounter a broad variety of levels of commitment, all of which will probably fall short of any picture of the 'ideal believer'. To claim to be a Roman Catholic, for example, may be a statement about racial or cultural origins, about the event of the administering of the sacrament of baptism, about a personal commitment to regular worship within the Catholic community. To be a Catholic may involve a wide diversity of commitment and belief: a lapsed Catholic may well be a professing atheist, yet still a Catholic in the eyes of the Church. The advent of a secular society has drawn religion into a sociological ambiguity. How does genuine belief relate to forms of common, folk and civic religion?

In a similar way, the ideal morality of a religious system may not be reflected in the actual practice of believers, both individually and collectively. We have to dig deep in telling the story of the history of Christianity to find a practical embodiment of the central virtue of Christian love; we have to look beyond its history of antisemitism and its, at least partial, responsibility for the Nazi holocaust; beyond its persecutions and crusades; beyond its support for the slave trade; beyond its misused power and wealth.

Again, we struggle to find an embodiment of the 'ideal' belief system. What, for example, is it exactly that Christians believe? Are we not faced with a long history of doctrinal disputes and conflicts? Is not the church fundamentally divided on what exactly it believes? Are there not Christian priests who claim to reconcile their Christianity with atheism? What constitutes true Christianity: Catholicism, Protestantism, Orthodoxy? In its conservative, liberal or radical forms?

To offer a picture of believers as those deeply committed to their faith, continuously putting that faith effectively into practice, and united in a 'common denominator' set of universally accepted beliefs is surely to offer an idealistic lie in the face of the realistic evidence. It is popular in classrooms to study the 'heroes' and 'heroines' of faith: we may now avoid David Livingstone on ideological grounds, but Mother Teresa, Gandhi, Martin Luther King and even, believe it or not, Bob Geldorf, remain popular figures. These idealized portraits do little justice to the complex realities of religious belief, and have of necessity to be carefully filtered: do we, for example, introduce children to the ambiguity surrounding Martin Luther King's marriage? Are we honest enough to look behind the myth and explore the reality? Has not the religious educator the duty to offer the pupil access to the real alongside the ideal if any depth at all of understanding is to be attained?

The function of religion

A common assumption in both confessional and liberal forms of religious education is that religion, in whatever form, has a positive function at both individual and collective levels. But the claim that religion automatically enhances the positive growth and development of individuals and society is at best a dubious one.

On the one hand the story can be told of how religion offers meaning and truth to humankind; how the prophets and religious leaders of the past were able to challenge the immorality of society, and provide a sense of purpose and meaning to believers. Our society, the story continues, is desperately in need of a similar spiritual rejuvenation, whether this involves a return to traditional Christian values or of the virtues of an open liberal society.

The alternative story is one of religion's complicity in human decay and stagnation; of the malaise forced on individuals expected to adopt a belief system that is essentially false and illusional; of the harm that religion inflicts on individuals and society; of the way religion breeds sectarian strife. The vision of a religion-less world, where denominational bigotry, stifling dogma, and misused religious authority are things of the past, where there is indeed, to quote from a popular English folk song, 'no hell below us, above us only sky', is for many an emancipating and genuinely moral one.

I have been able to do no more here than merely hint at the diversity and complexity of current attitudes towards religion. Though I have no doubt that many readers will dispute much of what I have said, it is the necessity of this dispute that lies at the heart of this section. All the various options outlined have long and highly intellectually respectable roots. None, I believe, can be simply dismissed out of hand, though most probably do need to be rejected in an intelligent way. Whether we like it or not, religion is a source of ambiguity and controversy. Whatever our own belief, however much we oppose alternative positions, we cannot deny the fact that these alternatives exist.

The value of ambiguity

The acceptance of complexity and ambiguity in the field of religious education is not an irritating inconvenience but rather a positive and necessary prerequisite of religious literacy.

At this stage it is easy to imagine objections from teachers: 'Getting pupils to settle down to work in religious education lessons can be difficult enough as it is. If we offer them material steeped in confusion rather than clarity surely it will become impossible?'. The objection is a serious one, raising as it does the crucial question of motivation.

Motivation

As teachers we are aware that the level of challenge offered to students in the classroom is crucial to their motivation. Offer a task that is too simple, a hurdle that is set too low, and interest and concentration quickly disappear: it is a simple task to complete the work whilst chatting with your friends about the events of last Saturday night. In the same way, offer a challenge that is too difficult, set the hurdle at an impossibly high level, and frustration and the overwhelming feeling of inadequacy will quickly turn students off from their allotted task. The result of getting the hurdles wrong is often the popular dismissal of a task as 'boring', in reality a cypher for 'too easy' or 'too difficult'. What is needed is a challenge that is a genuine one, but nevertheless is capable of being achieved.

I would suggest that much contemporary religious education sets the hurdles too low, and that this is a key reason for its failure. It can be a sobering experience to compare the expectations made in GCSE religious education papers with those of other subjects: somewhere along the line the former seems to have jettisoned its academic integrity. Learning what the inside of a mosque looks like is irrelevant if the key questions as to the meaning and truth of Islam are not addressed. An acceptance of ambiguity in the classroom will enable teachers to offer pupils genuine challenge, without the necessity of descending into confusion, provided it is handled skilfully and sensitively.

The justification of the place of ambiguity in the classroom goes beyond this extrinsic argument concerning the level at which the subject is pitched. As any teacher knows, genuine motivation must be rooted in an intrinsic interest in the subject. The twin issues of ambiguity and truth, I would suggest, actually offer pupils a way into a realization of the intrinsic value of studying religion. They ask questions that are of fundamental importance in the development of our humanity.

The intrinsic value of religious education

The suggestion that confusion and challenge lies at the heart of the development of insight and understanding is often reflected in our own lives. We have all, at some time or other, found ourselves forced out of the rut we have grown content to live in by an individual or an incident that forces us to reassess our values, beliefs and life styles; we have all faced challenges that threw us into uncertainty and placed a question mark over our assumptions; we have all come, at least in retrospect, to value the person or event as someone or something that enabled us to grow and develop as human beings.

So too, society. What community has not had need of its revolutionaries, its artists, its prophets whose challenge to the status quo has forced it to re-evaluate the direction it was travelling in? What society has not reacted with anger and indignation at the way in which such figures have challenged and made ambiguous the status quo, only for history, with the benefit of hindsight, to treat them as heroes, heroines and liberators?

Stewart Sutherland (1984) has drawn attention to the 'borderlands' between one's beliefs and the questioning of those beliefs: that territory in which certainty is replaced by ambiguity; where human growth and the realization of human potential becomes possible; where safety becomes danger; where we are forced to leave the security of our domesticity and move a stage further in the pilgrimage of our lives.

As teachers it seems to me that we constantly underestimate our pupils: the age of adolescence, of the passage from childhood to adulthood represents one of the, if not *the*, key 'borderlands' in all our lives. It is the time when students leave the security of their upbringing and begin to appropriate meaning, belief and life-style for themselves, on their own terms. They are, I believe, only too aware that religion constitutes a fundamental ambiguity in modern society. They know that atheism, agnosticism and religious belief are all viable options for adult life. Consequently, they see through the confessional Christian and liberal humanistic agendas of their teachers, and are fully aware that the picture of religion they are asked to adopt is only one of a broad range of options. By bringing truth and ambiguity to the classroom, it is possible to bypass these problems and thus allow students insight into the intrinsic importance and value of religious issues.

Education tends to be conservative, seeking all too often to pass on and preserve the security of the status quo. But why should education not be a force for change, not through the paternalistic imposition of solutions to the problem of religion proposed by a particular sub-group within society, but by embracing ambiguity in such a way that individuals and groups learn to take responsibility for themselves and for the nurturing and growth of the stories and traditions that they adhere to and have made their own? Why not allow individuals and groups to become religiously literate, to take the exhilarating risk of exploring their own borderlands, to embark for themselves on their own pilgrimage towards meaning, accompanied by others from their own and from other alternative traditions? Why not, indeed, introduce the positive and emancipatory reality of religious ambiguity into the classroom?

What do the aims of religious education look like once religious ambiguity is taken seriously? Since the 1988 Act there seems little doubt that educational theory has taken a politically-motivated pragmatic turn, and further that there is at least some consensus among political parties on this matter. We have learnt to expect from our education system a literate, skilled workforce, capable of providing the foundations of a long-term investment in the future wealth and prosperity of the nation. Hard-nosed practical pragmatism has replaced the soft-centred liberal idealism of the 1970s and early 1980s.

Beyond pragmatism

This situation presents problems for religious education. A few years ago I overheard a classroom conversation that went something like this: 'Miss, why do I have to do RE? I don't want to be a monk or priest or anything like that when I leave school'. 'Well, it can be useful if you want to go into one of the caring professions, you know, nursing or social work, something like that'. An improvement, I admit, on my own first attempt to answer the question: 'Because the law says you have to', but one cannot but help thinking that there is something missing here.

To utilize religious education to bring about moral rejuvenation and progress assumes that society already knows the future direction it needs to go in. This seems to me to be a false assumption, putting the cart before the horse. Does it not rather need to educate a new generation of democratic citizens who are capable of taking the debate on the future direction of society forward in an intelligent and informed way?

Religious education tends to adopt an immanent view of the world. Reality is all that we see and hear now, and our task is to live as quietly and as comfortably as we can within it. However, the religious question raises the issue of transcendence, of whether or not there is some transcendent deity or power from which our lives on earth should take their direction and meaning. Put another way, religious education is dealing with questions of intrinsic religious value and importance that may well precede the extrinsic question of personal and social development.

What comes out of these arguments is the impression that the subject has sought to justify itself by accepting a set view of the world and attempting to accommodate itself to this in order to gain legitimacy. In this it has shown no faith in its own intrinsic importance and value, nor in the possibility that society can learn from it by developing the ability to ask the religious questions of itself. What ultimately is true about ourselves, our values, our society, the universe we have been thrown into, and what are the implications of this for our educational system? In other words, the aim of religious education need be no more complicated than the process of producing religiously literate individuals. This is an aim in itself that has intrinsic importance and has no further need of justification.

Truth and humanization

We only have a short span of years on this earth, and if life has any value at all then it surely is fundamentally important how we go about the process of living. Someone gets up every Sunday and goes to church, staking their whole lives on the existence of not any God, but the God of Christianity, incarnate in Jesus. Someone else lies in bed, washes the car, plays squash or visits their in-laws on the assumption that there is no God. One of these two, or possibly even both, are living under an illusion, grounding their whole existence on a set of beliefs that are fundamentally wrong, living a life out of tune with what is ultimately true about humanity and our universe.

So too at the social level: one country bases its political system on the assumption that matters of religious belief are essentially private, and denies that the religious question has any role to play in the political process; another sets up an Islamic state, on the assumption that the claims of Allah in the Qur'an are at the heart of all reality. Again, one of these, if not both, are rooted in fundamentally false premises.

What I am suggesting in all this is that questions of truth precede questions of individual and social morality, that we cannot expect religious education to contribute to the extrinsic needs of society unless it is allowed to do so on its own terms, by asking the intrinsic question of religious truth.

The ultimate questions, of the true nature of reality are, then, of vital importance. If Socrates is right, and the unexamined life is indeed not worth living, then we need desperately to break out of our tunnel vision that causes us to opt for the short-term gratification of the easy solutions rooted in unexamined presuppositions, and to broaden our vision. We need to gain the courage to allow our humanity to develop, and the humanity of the next generation, by being willing to ask the difficult, long-term, ultimate questions.

It is also important to realize that these questions are not, in the long-term, avoidable. All life-styles and life-stances are rooted in some form of belief. Atheism, agnosticism and religious belief are all ultimately commitments to a particular understanding of the nature of reality. The liberal consensus in our present society that suggests that religious belief is a private, optional and unimportant extra is itself the embodiment of a particular set of beliefs about the nature of reality. If these and other beliefs are not put onto the educational agenda and questioned, then we allow our pupils to remain enslaved to a particular world view, without the skills or insight to investigate it further. We breed contented pigs, not discontented philosophers.

I am not suggesting that religious education, in adopting as its fundamental aim that of allowing pupils to become religiously literate, to be able to think, act and communicate intelligently about the ultimate questions that religion asks, can offer answers. The reality of religious ambiguity means that at present our society has no single answer; it is pluralistic, there are many answers, not all of which are true, not all of which are necessarily false. The subject has no right to pre-package the finished product, only to insist that students, whatever belief they adopt, do so in an informed and intelligent way. Thus the aim of a religious education that focuses on the question of religious truth, must be primarily concerned with process not results. It is possible to be a religiously illiterate atheist, agnostic and religious believer. I believe it is preferable to produce a society populated by religiously literate atheists, agnostics and believers.

By rejecting religious illiteracy, by embracing the reality of religious ambiguity and the value of exploring the issues this raises, religious education can learn to see itself as a subject of intrinsic value in itself, no longer parasitical on a particular world view, but rather in a position to offer society and individuals a set of skills, insights and perspectives that can only enhance the quality of our existence as human beings. If this causes uncertainty and questioning, all well and good, since to deny the value of this challenge is surely to deny the value of our humanity and of the universe we inhabit.

CHAPTER 5

Making Sense of Religion

On pigs and philosophers

One of the highlights of my present job is to have the privilege to sit at the back of classrooms and observe student teachers taking their first, sometimes confident, sometimes hesitant, steps along the path of their chosen profession. Our conversation afterwards will normally begin by concentrating on the technical aspects of the lesson: classroom management, organization, discipline and the like. Once these basics have been dealt with we are able to turn to more fundamental matters: how did the lesson serve to develop the religious understanding of pupils? What was the education process they were asked to go through? How can we help develop in children a religious literacy?

Increasingly I find myself encountering one of two different responses to these questions. One response reveals a student teacher with a clearly defined agenda. The nature of religion is seen as essentially simple and unproblematic, as is the reason why it is being taught. Such a teacher has already sorted out the classroom; religion has been pre-packaged for the easy consumption of the pupils. Implicitly, such a teacher has adopted a role somewhat similar to that of the tourist guides one sees in all the major European cities. Faced with a group of sightseers new to the city, the guide knows exactly which stories to tell, which quarters of the city to avoid. The tourists follow behind in an enthusiastic crocodile, camera shutters clicking: today Paris, tomorrow Berlin.

Such an approach seems to me to be responsible for much of the current malaise in religious education. It is essentially a 'safety first' policy that neutralizes the cutting edge of religion, denying it its dynamism, strength and controversial nature. It offers a superficial guide, a set of stereotypes, in a form that is essentially paternalistic. Most pupils, I believe, see through this 'tourist guide' approach. They are aware, through their upbringing, their contact with their peers, their perceptions of different attitudes within the school to the subject, and via the media, that religion is a controversial issue. To be asked blandly to look at, and appreciate, the phenomenon of religion does not allow them to address the critical questions they are already asking, at least implicitly, about the subject. They sense the dishonesty of what is on offer, and that sense leads to suspicion, frustration and boredom.

A second, and I am glad to say increasingly common response, reveals a student teacher with a much more open agenda. The ambiguity of religion, the disputes about its meaning, nature and truth, are brought into the classroom as problems to be addressed by the pupils themselves. There is no one solution to the religious questions on the agenda, rather a plurality of possible, yet contradictory, ways forward. There is an expectation that pupils should be challenged, and at the same time develop the skills to begin to find their own ways through the maze. The only precondition is that they do this in an informed, sensitive and educated manner. Implicitly, this style of teacher acts not so much as a tourist guide but as a host overseeing a prolonged sojourn in a city. The stranger is offered the opportunity to reside there for a while, to learn at first hand something of the language, customs, culture and way of life. Here the visitor is free to wander from the tourist routes, and explore the richness and complexity that lies at the heart of the hustle and bustle of modern urban life.

These two approaches to teaching bring us back to the two possible roads along which religious education may choose to travel. If we are to take seriously religious ambiguity and truth then we can no longer take the route of a safe, trouble-free journey to a prearranged destination. We must rather, like pilgrims, take the risk of straying from the highway, exploring side roads that may lead us to dead ends, but at the same time just might bring us to encounters that will challenge and reformulate our understanding of ourselves and our universe.

Religious education, I am suggesting, must learn to rediscover its sense of exploration and discovery and the exhilaration and danger this involves. Above all, it is a sense that the pupils themselves must be enabled to take on board and work with. When introducing pupils to this idea I used to ask them to make a choice between the two pigs in the following parable. Which pig would they rather be?

> There were once two pigs. They had lived all their life in a
> pigsty with tall brick walls, walls too high to see over. They

lived a contented existence, lying on their backs in the mud, sunbathing, watching a little television, keeping up with the latest fashions in designer pig wear and so on. Then one day a bolt of lightning struck the side of their enclosure. The first pig ignored the gaping hole opening up a path to the outside world. Why should he bother to go outside? Life inside was comfortable, safe and secure. The second pig was a little more restless. Plucking up courage she left the pigsty and began to explore. As she travelled on she encountered many things; some delighted her, others confused her; some made her frightened, others made her laugh. She became a pilgrim in a land she had never known, yet her fascination soon gave way to a thirst to find some kind of meaning in all she had experienced. She had many questions that needed answering. Then one day she encountered, sitting on a fence, a wise old owl. 'Can you tell me how to make sense of the world?', she asked. The owl was silent for a while, then finally looked up and replied, 'There is only one thing I can say to you: you must either stay here and remain a discontented philosopher, or return to your home and be a contented pig'.

Pupil-centred learning

If religious education is essentially a pilgrimage towards the truth and meaning of our humanity and our universe, then it is vital that in our exploration we bring our whole selves to the enterprise. Anything else will reduce religious education to some form of impersonal, academic, and hence irrelevant, enterprise.

Pupils coming to the religious education classroom will bring with them a set of attitudes, beliefs, perceptions and understandings of religion and its truth and relevance. True, these are unlikely to be developed in any structured, or even coherent, way, but nevertheless they form the starting point of any education that can make the claim of being 'pupil-centred'. Through the primary socialization of their home, and the secondary socialization of their peers, schooling and encounters with the media and outside worlds, students will inevitably approach the subject with a set of presuppositions, prejudices, assumptions and questions.

Religious education between 1944 and 1988 almost totally rejected the value and importance of this 'pre-knowledge'. We have seen how *confessionalism* failed to take account of the reality of the post-Christian religious situation in Britain in 1944, and approached education within a 'postal-worker' model in which the teacher's role was essentially one of posting packets of knowledge into empty minds. The *explicit/phenomenological* approach, in its desire to remain neutral and objective, required students to suspend their judgements and prejudices, to put them to one side and approach religion with a clean slate, an empty mind.

The *implicit* and *spiritual* models of religious education did make the attempt to start from the pupils' own perspectives, to be genuinely student-centred. However, they fell into the trap of ignoring the personal histories and biographies of pupils. The starting point was not that of the paths they had travelled on to reach the particular understanding of religion they brought to the classroom; not that of their relationship, or lack of relationship, to a particular religious community; not that of the religious attitudes they had picked up in their homes and in society. No, all this was placed to one side and seen in some way as being irrelevant or even detrimental to the learning process.

In its place was put the notion of an ahistorical notion of 'experience'. The starting point of religious education was seen in terms of the pupils' ability to be sensitive towards their own inner lives, their 'inner space', and their appreciation of the awe and wonder generated by religious phenomena. Pupils' failure to appreciate and be sensitive towards religion on these terms was not put down to the reality that for many of them their upbringing had led them to view religion as a remnant of a past superstitious age that had no relevance to their lives and could make no truth claims about the universe. Rather, the problem was seen in terms of a perceived lack of sensitivity towards the spiritual dimension itself, the result of a society which, under the influence of a science utilized in pragmatic and technological ways, had become essentially materialistic and blind to any other dimension of life.

It became commonplace to argue that, prior to religious education taking place, pupils must be 'sensitized' towards a spiritual dimension that they were not capable of appreciating for themselves. The consequence of this was that even a religious education that claimed to start from where the pupils themselves were, began by denying the value, importance and reality of the understanding of religion they brought to the classroom. From the start, their beliefs were seen as inadequate because they lacked sensitivity towards the world and themselves.

If we do begin with the actual attitudes that pupils bring to the classroom, and allow them the freedom and space to be open and honest (even if this means allowing the possibility of a negative attitude to be expressed in the classroom) then religious education can allow them to embark on the pilgrimage on their own terms, with the security of being allowed to articulate and explore their own points and beliefs. The pilgrimage of religious education thus can become one in which the pupils take part in an ongoing dialogue between the ambiguity of the truth claims of religion and their own developing self-understanding, beliefs and world view.

The aim then becomes that of finding ways of enabling them to develop their own beliefs, and their understanding of the beliefs of others, in an increasingly intelligent and informed manner. Given the conflicting understandings of religion present in our society, it is surely illegitimate that religious education rules out any single attitude or belief *a priori,* yet at the same time entirely legitimate to expect that, as education progresses, whatever beliefs are held are held in an increasingly literate manner.

Exploring religion

How are pupils to be taught religion in the context of a personally-focused pilgrimage in search of the truth about themselves and their universe? How are the religious issues to be presented to them? In adopting the now traditional model of 'knowledge', 'understanding' and 'evaluation', I do not want to give the impression that these three areas can be separated out one from another, nor to suggest that religious understanding takes place via a progression in which knowledge is received, then understood and then evaluated in a neat, structured way. It is important to see the three in a holistic way, as inter-linked circles, and to appreciate that the complex process of understanding takes place on all three levels simultaneously. It is extremely dangerous to allow an interpretative framework such as this one to become the basis for a teaching method itself, as happens in some classrooms, when, for example, pupils are instructed that a particular GCSE project is a 'knowledge-based' one, or an 'understanding-focused' one, or an 'evaluative' one!

Religious knowledge

Given this word of warning, how is it possible to go about introducing pupils to a knowledge of religion that takes account of both the reality of ambiguity and the question of truth? I would like to suggest that it involves us rethinking the *scope*, the *depth* and the

70

interpretative framework by which religion is currently offered in our classrooms.

Scope

Between 1944 and 1988 religious education, in terms of its perception of the scope of the subject, moved from one extreme to the other. It began with an exclusive focus on a narrowly-defined Christianity, and by 1988 was offering a full-scale introduction to the now famous 'big six' world religions (Buddhism, Christianity, Hinduism, Islam, Judaism and Sikhism). One of the prime motivations for this shift was the desire of the religious education industry to show itself to be balanced and neutral. This could only be achieved, it was assumed, if equal weight and time were given to each religion. What in fact had happened was that the issue of multicultural politics had taken precedence over the issue of education itself.

Let us for a moment put the political question on one side, and adopt an educational perspective. If we want to introduce children to the riches of the tradition of English literature we do not set out to give them a birds' eye view of all the major writers, but select out a few key texts to investigate in depth. If we want to introduce children to Shakespeare on the stage we take them to see a single play, we do not lose sleep over not having taken them to see them all. There is a play currently doing the rounds in London that offers the whole Shakespeare corpus, abridged of course, in the space of two hours: it is, though, a comedy. Educational concerns thus demand that depth be given preference over breadth.

The current scope of the content of religious education is so broad that it inevitably leads to superficiality and the lack of any possibility of any genuine depth of religious understanding. What is required is a careful selection of topics, based on an acceptance of the impossibility of covering everything, and rooted in a criterion that is justified on educational rather than political grounds.

Such decisions about the content of the curriculum need, of course, to reflect the fact that Christianity is the major religious tradition within Britain, whilst at the same time taking account of other religious systems. I would suggest that a reasonable balance would involve the combination of four key perspectives. First, pupils will need to develop a picture of the interrelationship between the various traditions they encounter. Thus religious education will need to involve a basic introduction to all the major religions as part of the process of building a basic groundwork. Second, Christianity needs to be a religious tradition that is studied in genuine depth. Third, a major non-Christian religious tradition will need to be explored at a comparable level. The decision as to which one would need to take into account local circumstances. Fourth, these would need to be compared and contrasted with the reality of the possibility of a non-religious understanding of humanity and the universe, such as has developed in western culture since the Enlightenment. This is of particular importance: the desire to be balanced has all too often been linked with the desire to encourage pupils to appreciate the value of religion, but if we are to take ambiguity seriously then the importance of non-religious claims to truth cannot possibly be ignored.

Depth

Given a more limited, though still balanced, scope of the content of the subject, we are now free to introduce a level of depth in our approach to religion, to move beyond the superficiality of a mere birds' eye viewpoint. But what exactly do we mean by religious depth? How is it to be found? Where is it located?

Since the 1960s religious educators have offered a highly influential, but I believe fundamentally misguided, answer to this question, namely that any depth of understanding of religious traditions is to be found in the religious experience held to underpin religious phenomena. There is operating here a particular model of religion, an 'experiential-expressive' one: religion is rooted in the religious experience of humankind, an experience that is given a variety of different expressions through various historical and cultural religious traditions. Thus to get to the heart of religion it is necessary to move beyond the cultural expression of religion, the religious phenomena, and focus on the religious experience that is at its centre.

The model has its roots in the western tradition. The Enlightenment, with its mistrust of the authority of traditions and its stress on the importance of human reason, denied that the authority of a religious text or community offered a path to religious truth. At the same time it also denied that religion could be based on human reason alone. The German theologian Schleiermacher, in the last century, turned to the category of experience as a foundation for religion, since the paths of religion based on reason or the authority of scripture or church had been denied him. Religions, he claimed, have their heart in humanity's experience of God, an experience given articulation in a variety of historical religious traditions.

The problem with this is that such a model does not do justice to the way religions actually understand themselves. Ask a Muslim where the heart of Islam lies, and they will reply Allah's revelation to humanity contained in the Qur'an, rather than the experience of Muslim believers. Similarly, traditional Christianity draws its heart from a belief in God's revelation in becoming human in the incarnation, through the life and teaching of Jesus, not from the religious experience of Christians. The religions themselves point to the public, objective truth claims they make about reality, not to private, subjective experience, when asked to speak about what lies at their heart.

The heart of religion lies, then, in the claims to truth it makes about the objective nature of the universe and the place of society and individuals within this world view. To reach a depth of understanding of religion thus involves not achieving insight into religious experience, but reaching an understanding of the world view a religion holds, of its specific claims to religious truth. It is the teaching of religions, their concrete beliefs, and the question of the coherence and truth of these claims that marks the heart of religion, as it is understood by believers themselves.

Interpretative framework

When presenting pupils with religious knowledge, I am suggesting we need to focus in depth on the truth claims of a limited number of conflicting religious and non-religious systems, not to look superficially at the phenomena and religious experience of all. This inevitably requires an ability to portray conflicting truth claims in the classroom, and hence of adopting an interpretative framework for religions that does justice to their diverse and conflicting natures.

This, as I have already argued, involves addressing in the classroom an ambiguity that religious education has tried systematically to avoid. The desire to give a neutral picture is linked to a misunderstanding about the nature of teaching. To teach something, it is wrongly assumed, is to advocate it. The teacher here is placed in the role of 'expert', the one with the answers to the ambiguity of religion. Because religious beliefs contradict, teachers asked to play this role, and seeking desperately to avoid any appearance of bias, offer a bland picture of the 'facts' in any interpretative framework that, it is hoped, will be acceptable to all religious traditions.

If we can get away from the idea that to teach is to advocate, and see the teacher as a fellow pilgrim in the search for meaning and truth, then the necessity of coming up with the 'right' answer, by which is meant a bland non-committed one acceptable to all, is taken off the agenda. The true role of the teacher is that of educator, of bringing pupils to a deeper and increasingly literate understanding of the nature of religion. Such a teacher will want to present the ambiguities of religion as a necessary part of this learning process. That the 'true' answer remains an open question is simply not a problem, since in our present pluralistic society there is no one, generally accepted, religious 'truth'. What matters is not the results, but the quality of the learning process itself.

Religious understanding

Presenting knowledge of religion in the classroom thus involves an in-depth study of selected topics in a way that draws attention both to the heart of the claims religions make to truth, and to the disputed and controversial nature of these truth claims when viewed from the perspective of different traditions. The question now to be asked is how, given the presentation of such information, pupils may be helped to begin to make sense of the claims and counter-claims for themselves? How might they be helped to reach an understanding of this religious knowledge?

The traditional answer, linked to the belief that it is religious experience, not truth claims, that lies at the heart of religion, is that of the process of 'empathy'. Once the religious phenomenon has been objectively described, the process of understanding involves the development of an ability to put oneself in the shoes of the believer, to experience the world imaginatively in the way the believers themselves do, since it is in the experience of believers that truth of religion actually lies, we are told. The Christian Education Movement brought out a series of videos in the 1980s that attempted to do just that. Videos with titles such as 'Judaism Through the Eyes of Jewish Children' made clear the centrality of empathy as a means of reaching understanding.

Though I would not want to dispute that empathy has a part to play in the learning process, if it stands alone it is surely inadequate. What exactly does one do once one has imagined oneself as a Muslim at prayer, or as present at a Christian Baptism? Empathy simply leaves all the crucial questions unanswered, all the conflicting stories unexplored. Religious educators seem content to ignore this challenge and instead devise increasingly strange and elaborate ways of accomplishing empathy with pupils. My favourite is the following:

> Pesach is a religious festival when Jews thank God (sic) for their escape from Egypt. They believe God (sic) controls the world and its history. These are important ideas. Many Jews believe that to celebrate properly, the home must be carefully prepared. It is important that no leaven should be found in the house. For the strictest families this means that the house must be spring-cleaned (Fageant and Mercer, 1988, p.63).

All well and good. The stage has been set for pupils to being to grapple with the claims made by Judaism. Perhaps we will be asked to look at the Biblical texts that tell the Exodus story and begin to understand them a little better. Or will we perhaps pick up the idea of G-d controlling history and explore the truth of Jewish beliefs about divine providence and the Jewish nation as G-d's chosen people? And surely the assumption made in the question that belief in G-d's action in the world is 'important' is a highly controversial one to which many pupils would respond with a resounding 'no': may we assume that it has been placed there as a means of generating classroom debate? No, the idea that experience and not truth claims lies at the heart of religion prevails: we must get back to the religious experience of Jews preparing to celebrate Pesach. What task will be allotted us to help develop our understanding of Judaism?

> Write out a plan of how you would set about fully cleaning your home, remembering especially any spots where crumbs of food might be trapped (DES, 1988, Section 1, 2).

Quite apart from the inadequate way the question portrays Judaism, must we not question the adequacy of such an approach, drawn, incidentally, from a particularly popular textbook that claims a concern to develop pupils' 'skills' in understanding religion? How can it hope to increase students' religious literacy? What does it say about the intellectual and academic integrity of the subject?

If not through empathy and imagination, how are we to develop in pupils an understanding of religious issues? It is all too easy to complicate matters here, to see religious understanding as some kind of mystical, subjective, even gnostic process. I would argue that the issue is essentially a very simple one. If I want to discover the extent of a pupils' religious education I would not attempt anything more mysterious than to listen to them articulating their understanding of religion. What is the quality of their ability to have an intelligent and literate conversation about religion? How far are they able to put into words their insights into the complexity and ambiguities surrounding the subject? How far are they capable of offering a reasoned and intelligent description of their own beliefs concerning religion? Rather than a model of religious understanding rooted in 'emphatic insight', we need to move towards a model based on 'linguistic competence'.

The methods for achieving this are to be found in the skills and disciplines that have been developed in faculties of theology and religious studies in universities and institutes of higher education. It is there that we can tap into a centuries-long tradition of developed linguistic skills for the study of religion, to repair the rupture between religion and scholarship.

Pupils need to be introduced to these skills and disciplines: of course at an appropriate level, but nevertheless religious education in schools needs to see itself as part of that whole academic tradition. Scholars working in this area have long used a variety of disciplines as aids to the interpretation of religion: literary and textual criticism, historical criticism, sociology, psychology and anthropology. At the heart are the twin disciplines of theology and of philosophy of religion. If we want students to become religiously literate, to develop the linguistic competence of understanding religion, then we cannot fight shy of once again introducing an academic foundation to religious education.

I do not see this suggestion as being any different than the approach to secondary education adopted by any other subject. History teachers seek to enable pupils to take their first steps in mastering the discipline of historical study; English teachers look to introduce their pupils to the skills of literary criticism — so why should religious educators not seek to produce fledgling theologians and religious philosophers? Why is such an aim so often reserved for those who choose to study the subject at A-level? In seeking to understand religion there is surely little alternative to taking on board the academic tradition that makes this possible.

Evaluating religion

Alongside the development of knowledge of religion and the linguistic competences required to understand this knowledge, stands the need to evaluate the religious issues. This is demanded of pupils by agreed syllabuses and the GCSE examination boards, yet given the current state of play of religious education it seems to me at present to be an impossible task. There are a number of factors that block any serious attempt to begin to evaluate the claims and counter-claims of religious and non-religious beliefs.

First, the demand for neutrality. Liberal religious education, in its desire to be unbiased, has insisted on neutral presentation in the classroom. Since all are offered as having equal value, there seems to be no way in which judgements between them can be made by pupils.

Second, the expectation that pupils come to appreciate the value of religion. Despite the introduction in the Birmingham Agreed Syllabus in the 1970s of Marxism and Humanism as legitimate fields of study, religious education has tended to avoid any space for exploration of objections to religious belief. Though no longer concerned to bring children to a specific faith, teachers still remain concerned to instil in pupils an appreciation of an assumed value in religious belief.

This is presumably linked to a concern on their part to justify the subject: 'Although you may not see it now, in fact there is great value in the religious traditions'. This ignores, of course, a fundamentally important strand in the development of human understanding of religion. The value of religious education lies, as we have argued, not in the value of religious responses to the questions the universe and our humanity throw out to us, but in the importance of the questions themselves, regardless of whether they are given a religious or non-religious answer. The result of this desire to insist on religious value is that judgements made by students in this context are necessarily limited by a need to be positive about religious belief. A child who is developing, quite legitimately if we are taking pluralism seriously, a negative response to religious answers to ultimate questions, finds their perspective an unacceptable one within the framework in which the class is being asked to work.

Third, the way in which religious belief has been privatized. If religious belief is purely subjective, and can make no claim to public knowledge, then the process of evaluation becomes an impossible one, since there are no public criteria on which to make judgements. As a result, a child being asked to evaluate religious questions is able to do no more than express a personal preference, and will not be able to justify that preference further than suggesting that it is the one they 'like'.

This links up with the liberal concept of freedom of belief. If all beliefs, provided they tolerate the beliefs of others, are legitimate, then we fall into the trap of believing that there is no way of making informed judgements in this area. Because we cannot arrive at public certainty, we mistakenly assume that we must move to the other extreme of some form of anarchic freedom. The reality, of course, is that we are coming to realize that almost all our claims to knowledge are in some way contingent. Whether judging between scientific disputes between expanding and steady-state theories of the universe, the relative qualities of the music of Mozart and the Rolling Stones, or the literary merits of Graham Green and Dostoyevsky, we make informed and critical judgements based on the best evidence available. Each judgement will be disputed by others, but so long as it is an informed one, based on evidence, insight and wisdom, and so long as it is open to being adapted in the light of further knowledge and understanding, then it quite legitimately takes its place in the ongoing intellectual pilgrimage and conversation of humankind.

However, this notion of critical judgement, together with the skills and understanding it requires, is not something that religious educators have sought to impart to pupils. When asked to evaluate religious material they are forced to work in a vacuum. If their teachers are insisting that all religions are equally valid, are rejecting the view that there might be no positive value in religious belief, and are suggesting that religious faith is essentially a private affair in which 'anything goes' provided it does no harm to others, how then is the pupil to proceed when asked to make judgements? The inevitable result is surely that they express their own personal preference, and then hit a brick wall. The development of their own belief becomes a matter of personal taste, and no more. This is a situation resulting from bad education, that can only add to the reality of religious illiteracy. It leaves children adrift on a rudderless raft, fine prey for the religious charlatans who are such a feature of contemporary society.

Yet paradoxically, the process of religious evaluation is an inevitable one. There is simply no way of avoiding making judgements on religious questions. To claim atheism, agnosticism or a particular form of religious commitment all involve an evaluation, however badly through-out and ill-considered. To simply avoid the religious question as irrelevant, in itself involves a judgement about religion.

Genuine, rather than superficial, tolerance also demands evaluation. To tolerate a religious faith on the grounds that 'I like it' simply falls into the trap of patronization. Further, to be expected to 'like' something in which one sees little value roots toleration in fundamentally dishonest premises. A genuine tolerance will have been prepared to investigate in depth, to reach a conclusion rooted in informed wisdom. Toleration with any level of moral integrity to it must begin with mutual recognition of, and acceptance of, differences as the basis for developing shared dialogue and understanding. This is, I believe, a crucial truth that the Muslim community in Britain can teach our pluralistic society.

It is, then, a key task for the teacher to enable pupils to make, in informed, sensitive and crucial ways, judgements on the material they are being asked to handle. The skills of philosophical and theological thinking are ones that pupils need to be helped to apply in weighing up the strengths and weaknesses of their own and other claims about the ultimate truth and meaning of our universe.

So long as this evaluation is done from the perspective of an increasingly literate approach to religious issues, then the actual content of their conclusions is of little or no importance; what matters is the quality of their appreciation of the ongoing search for meaning and truth.

On being religiously educated

From this discussion it is possible to begin to map out what criteria we may look for in a student who may legitimately make the claim of being 'religiously educated'.

They will have come to accept that the universe, society and their own humanity throws out fundamental and ultimate questions, the answers to which will fundamentally affect the way they approach their lives. Preferring the role of discontented philosopher to that of contented pig, they will be willing to set out to play their part in humanity's search for truth and meaning.

During this pilgrimage they will acknowledge and articulate their own answers to these ultimate questions, striving to reach a deeper understanding of them, and be willing to alter and adapt them should this become necessary.

They will develop a depth of knowledge of a number of key religious and non-religious belief systems that offer contrasting and conflicting answers to these ultimate questions.

This knowledge will be interpreted and understood using their developing skills of theological and philosophical reflection, by means of which they will come to take part in an ongoing process of evaluating the various claims to truth offered in answer to the ultimate questions humanity has to deal with.

The result will be pupils who have embarked on the journey towards increasing religious literacy, pupils increasingly able to think, speak and act in an intelligent way towards religious issues.

CHAPTER 6

Religion for Citizenship

Social and personal education

We have outlined a model of religious education rooted in the religious quest for the ultimate truth about the universe, society and ourselves, and suggested that this quest should take the form of enabling pupils to develop the reflective, linguistic and practical competences needed for the search to be carried out in a literate and educated way. We turn now to the question as to how such an intellectual and spiritual journey can help the social and personal development of pupils in our schools.

The 1988 Education Reform Act clearly puts the topic firmly on the educational agenda. We need do no more than to turn once again to that oft-quoted statement in the first section of the Act, which draws attention to the entitlement of children to a curriculum that

> promotes the spiritual, moral, cultural, mental and physical development of pupils...(and) prepares such pupils for the opportunities, responsibilities and experiences of adult life (DES, 1988, section 1, 2).

As well as the responsibility of individual subjects to play their particular roles in offering this entitlement, the whole curriculum also addresses cross-curricular elements that have direct relevance to the personal and social development of individual pupils. These include the *dimensions* of equal opportunities in the context of education for life, *skills* such as communication, and specified *themes* including careers guidance, health education and education for citizenship.

Since clearly the Act envisages education towards the personal, social, spiritual and moral development of the child as being something that flows through the whole of the educational process, encompassing the whole life of the school as a learning community and demanding input from all subject areas in addition to cross-curricular work, the inevitable task before us must be to ask the question of the distinctive nature of the role of religious education in all this.

We have already warned against the danger of religious education being utilized by schools in inappropriate ways in this regard. If the subject is to remain true to its primary function of addressing the issues of ultimate questions, of religious truth and of religious ambiguity, then it cannot allow religion simply to be utilized as a cement that binds a divided society together, whether in a confessional or a liberal form. Such cement will not stick. If the subject sells itself short in this matter then it will not be able to deliver that which it has to offer that is of genuine and unique worth.

This danger, though, is still firmly on the agenda, the result of the introduction by the 1988 Act of the vocabulary of 'spirituality' and 'spiritual development' and the recognition that social and personal development must in some form address this agenda. The language of spirituality is ambiguous: it has clear religious overtones, yet is entirely capable of being understood both in a confessional and in a broad liberal humanistic framework. Indeed the precedence for this had been set by the Inspectorate as early as 1977, when two contrasting definitions of the spiritual were offered (Grimmitt, 1987). One was a liberal humanistic perspective:

> The spiritual area is concerned with the awareness a person has of those elements in existence and experience which may be defined in terms of inner feelings and beliefs that affect the way people see themselves and throw light for them on the purpose and meaning of life itself (p.393).

The other was a theological perspective:

> The spiritual area is concerned with everything in human knowledge or experience that is connected with or derives from a sense of God or of Gods (p.393).

The contrast here clearly leaves room for religious education to continue the process of accommodation with, and assimilation towards, programmes of moral education rooted in either confessionalism or liberal humanism, programmes in which the specifically religious questions have only a marginal role to play. Is this another case of religious education allowing itself to swim with the tide in an effort to gain recognition and status? Has the subject nothing more specific to offer children and society?

A distinctive agenda for religious education?

What are the values that underpin an education for citizenship, and how do these relate to the specific responsibilities of religious education? The answer to these questions was left undefined by the 1988 Act. The 1992 White Paper, *Choice and Diversity* (DfE, 1992), building as it does on the framework of the Education Reform Act, attempts in some way to clarify the situation. Education, we are told 'cannot and must not be value-free', and therefore, 'at the heart of every school's educational and pastoral policy and practice should lie a set of shared values'. Furthermore, it is suggested, 'every attempt should be made to ensure that these values are endorsed by parents and the local community' (p.37). This seems a somewhat strange set of affairs: on the one hand there exists a set of shared values, values presumably so obvious that there is no need to articulate them, yet it seems to be assumed that there is a possibility that parents and the local community may not actually endorse them!

At this stage of the proceedings it is difficult not to indulge in the game of reading between the lines and speculating about the implicit assumptions made in the document as to the nature of these 'shared values'. At root there appears to be present a number of basic virtues: honesty, tolerance, respect, self-control, etc. On an individual level these virtues seem to help produce pupils who are rational, autonomous, well-integrated and with stable and pleasing personalities. Such personalities will enable pupils to enter adulthood equipped to become fulfilled, successful members of society with a clear aim and purpose in life.

But what exactly is the aim and purpose of life? By what measure do we gauge success? Possibly I am being a little over-cynical here, but is it not just possible that we get a hint of part of an answer in the following statement in the White Paper, extracted from the section on increased specialization and diversity in schools:

> The Government's first priority will be to continue to encourage specialisation in the teaching of technology, with particular emphasis on its vocational aspects, because it believes that the economic health of the country requires the vigorous promotion of technology in schools (DfE, 1992, p.44).

Is economic well-being one of the 'shared values' of our society? The rhetoric of politicians, advertisers and the media would seem to support an affirmative answer.

Yet one does not have to look far to find this notion being

questioned. A recent correspondent in the *Church Times* (2 October, 1992) felt the need to register his 'disgust' at 'the reduction of the Christian message to selfish individualism'. Put another way, have we a moral right, living as we do in the midst of the richest and most affluent culture known to humankind, to worry about *our* economic growth (as opposed to a fairer redistribution of the wealth we already have) while two-thirds of humanity starves below the bread line?

The point I am trying to make is not primarily a political one. I am rather suggesting that as soon as we begin to ask questions about issues such as the criteria for 'success' in life, or the ultimate purpose of our existence as human beings, we cannot but help start asking theological and religious questions. What, in the end, does it mean to be 'human'? Who am I? What is the meaning of life? How come there is 'something' rather than 'nothing'? If we do this, we come immediately across a plurality of possibilities, most of which are so contradictory that they force us to doubt the existence of a common shared set of values. It is illuminating to contrast the understanding of the nature of humanity which is (possibly) implicit in recent government legislation, with a Christian view of the nature and purpose of humanity.

Christians are called to discipleship, called to follow in the footsteps of Jesus of Nazareth. Living a life of abject poverty, with no home or possessions, that man died a failure in the eyes of the world. Rather than align himself with the rich and successful, he chose a nomadic existence, eating, drinking and sleeping with the outcasts, the moral and social failures of his society. He insisted over and over again that the way of discipleship led not to comfort and security, but to challenge, danger and persecution. His followers were asked to follow him with a cross on their shoulders, to have as their central symbol an instrument of execution. Furthermore, the qualification for discipleship lay not in any personal success or achievement, but rather in the ability to face up to and accept one's own inadequacies, brokenness and sin. The end of the journey was a relationship with God, not in any sense at all any material reward.

One is perhaps entitled to stop apologizing for being cynical when one reads in the White Paper that 'proper regard should continue to be paid to the nation's Christian heritage and traditions' (DfE, 1992, para. 8.2). Is this really what is meant, and if so why bother with City Technology Colleges? Apparently Christianity must be taken seriously, but not too seriously.

We seem to have arrived, yet again, at the issue of ambiguity. If we are concerned with the personal development of the pupils in the classroom, then as religious educators we must surely have the right, and indeed the duty, to place the question as to the ultimate destination of such development in a religious framework. It would be easy to supplement the descriptions above of a liberal humanistic and Christian concept of the end of humanity with other, equally contradictory models drawn from other religious and non-religious traditions.

In this context we as teachers have a simple choice. Do we utilize the religious content of our subject to support and affirm a single, implicit understanding of the purpose of humanity, whether that be the vision of confessionalists or liberals, and so once again swim with the tide in the hope of increased recognition of the importance and relevance of the subject? Or do we allow ourselves to suggest that the serious and intelligent study of the religious questions can only put a question mark over such assumptions? Cannot religious education contribute to the personal development of individual pupils precisely by insisting that they address for themselves, in an intelligent and informed manner, the ambiguous, yet deeply serious nature, of such questions?

Starting from shared values

Despite my rather cynical view of the way the following suggestion may have been intended to have been read, I would nevertheless give its core ideal unanimous support:

> Education cannot and must not be value-free...At the heart of every school's educational and pastoral policy and practice should lie a set of shared values (DfE, 1992, para. 8.3).

Education *cannot* be value-free, since to claim that pupils are free to choose their values for themselves is in reality an advocacy of the value of anarchy. Education *must* not be value-free, because to accept the value of anarchy is to accept the legitimate value of the holocaust. Personal freedom must have its limitations, or else we descend into an amoral society.

The reality of our moral development is that we learn our values by the way we interact with our environment and society. Whether children are mistreated and abused or loved and nurtured will inevitably have a profound effect on the way their values develop and the way they learn to act towards others in a moral or amoral way. This is not to suggest that environment alone is the sole source of a pupil's moral development, and that personal responsibility is not a key factor. Nevertheless, the acceptance of the need for the school to offer a set of shared values reflects the importance of environment in moral development. Moral and personal development has its roots in the way a pupil is nurtured within the shared values of the school community.

A good school will operate as a microcosm of society as a whole. The way in which the school organizes itself, the quality of its structures and the interpersonal relationships within these structures will be of primary importance. A school's ethos, the ways in which the school develops as a society of learners, the ways in which it responds to tensions and disputes — all these will contribute to a pupil's understanding of, and response to, society as a whole.

This, however, takes us only so far. We still have to overcome the problem of the reality of a plurality of, often conflicting, values in contemporary society. Despite this plurality, I would suggest that there are three ways for a school to move forward faced with this dilemma.

First, there does seem to exist a number of basic values that schools should adhere to, despite the reality of pluralism. The shared core virtues of honesty, tolerance, respect, self-control and so on should form the backbone of any school's life. These virtues will not solve all the problems a school will inevitably face in this area, and there will be a need to unpack them as the corporate life of the school develops. Nevertheless, we must start from somewhere.

Second, given the move towards increasing autonomy for schools, and their freedom to develop their own distinctive ethos, there would seem to be room for these virtues to be articulated in a number of different ways, dependent on the circumstances of a particular school. Thus these core virtues might be given a distinctive interpretation in schools founded within specific religious traditions, be they Anglican or Roman Catholic, Jewish or, possibly in the future, Muslim. Alternatively, schools in the state sector might appropriate these core virtues in a way which reflects the particular communities they serve, be they the values of a school in the inner city, or rural countryside.

Each individual school would then take on the responsibility of generating and articulating a set of shared values which draw on core virtues, but which are distinctive of their particular ethos and nature. That this involves the existence of schools with different shared values need not be a problem in itself: given the plurality of values in our society it is surely not inappropriate to expect all schools to utilize these common virtues in ways appropriate to their local situations. We cannot expect schools to compensate for society in this way, and in any case it is unclear whether a society developing in a morally healthy way actually requires a single set of values. Is there not a case for seeing a virtue in moral pluralism, of a restless search for better and more viable value systems? What matters is that each school contributes to the moral development of pupils by offering a stable and effective environment in which such development can take place.

Third, given that schools are essentially educational communities, should not the shared value of the educational process itself be found at the heart of every school? The shared value of the ongoing search for knowledge, the ongoing thirst for meaning, the ongoing pilgrimage by a community of learners towards a greater harmony with themselves, society and the environment? If such a search involves taking account of and making sense of a plurality of values, then the fact of moral pluralism becomes not a problem to be avoided but a fact of life to be appropriated and used as the very material through which moral and personal development takes place.

It is through the act of collective worship that the shared values and developing ethos of a school are to be celebrated and articulated according to the framework of the 1988 Act. The central importance of an assembly of the school community in which its life and values are celebrated seems to me to be of fundamental importance. The opportunity to draw the thread of the community's life together, to collectively rejoice over its achievements and face up to its failures is surely of paramount importance if a school is to make its shared values a reality.

In schools with a religious foundation it seems to me to be entirely appropriate, indeed essential, that this assembly involves an act of worship that reflects the particular religious tradition in which it stands. It is important, though, that such communities also have the courage in the midst of this worship to be honest about the inevitable plurality within it. The reality of staff in the school who are part of that community, but do not subscribe to its religious foundation and values, needs to be acknowledged, not by watering down the worship into something they can accept, but by recognizing their rightful place as participants within the school's life, though not as members of its faith tradition. So too the needs of pupils in the school who do not come from that particular faith community, or who come from an alternative tradition within that faith, or whose pilgrimage has taken them away from the beliefs of their parents who chose that particular school for them because of their own religious commitment. Worship in such a community needs to both hold fast to the celebration of its religious traditions whilst at the same time learning to be honest about the plurality within it.

In schools which have no formal allegiance to a religious tradition, the nature of any assembly celebrating its shared values is likely to be problematic if this assembly is interpreted as an act of collective worship. It is difficult to see how such an event cannot but help lead the school into hypocrisy, allowing a core of unreality and dishonesty to filter into the very heart of its life. Assembly as 'worship' is surely a contradiction in terms if the community's core values are not religious: not only does it become farcical, it also utilizes the worship of genuine believers in a form that can easily become disrespectful. An assembly that is in harmony with the values of the school, that is able to celebrate and rejoice in its collective ethos, is surely a more realistic alternative. Though the 1988 Act does offer some scope for creative management in this situation, the underlying legal requirement of collective worship is, as it stands, more likely to impair rather than nurture the development of a school's shared values.

Education for citizenship needs then to be rooted in the ongoing development of a school's ethos and environment that has as its heart core virtues articulated in a form which does justice to the individual character of the community as a learning community that is able to celebrate its nature with integrity through collective worship and assemblies.

What distinctive role is there in all this for the religious education department? To simply identify religion with morality and place the burden of this task on the religious education teacher, will only serve to compromise both the school and religious education itself. The task is surely one that all members of the school community, under the leadership of the headteacher, must take responsibility for. Religious education thus has a duty to participate fully in this collective task, by ensuring that the religious aspect of the school's ethos is dealt with appropriately and with integrity. There will be a need to insist that religion is not misused by utilizing it in inappropriate ways, and also to insist that its positive contribution is put in place in effective and creative ways.

Partnership across the curriculum

Given that the school community offers a nurturing environment in which effective moral and social development can take place, what place is there within the explicit curriculum for education for citizenship, and what should religious education's role be here? The first vital step is for religious educators to place clear limits on their role in such a process. The model I have in mind is of a partnership between religious education and the whole curriculum. There is a role for religious education, a role of fundamental importance, but this role cannot be extended to a situation in which religious education is given sole or even primary responsibility for moral education.

All departments, not just departments of religious education, need to accept responsibility for the future development of society. English, history, geography, science, indeed all subject areas will not be able to avoid these issues sooner or later appearing on their agendas. There can be no justification for any department avoiding these issues on the grounds that they are the domain of the religious education teacher. Morality, citizenship and multiculturalism are all essentially cross-curricular themes. Any good school will insist that at a minimum they are dealt with, as they arise, in all subject areas. Ideally it is reasonable to expect departments to go beyond this and make such issues specifically identifiable in their curriculums.

In many schools these themes will also appear directly in programmes of personal and social education, active tutorial work and the like. The flourishing of such programmes may be seen as a direct result of the realization that, in a plural society, it is not necessarily in order to equate morality with religion. They accept, by implication, the reality that for many in society morality is increasingly a secular issue, and not necessarily any the worse for being so.

Is is of vital importance that religious education avoids the trap of reductionism, that it does not by-pass its role of education in religion in favour of a possibly more comfortable role of moral educator. This is an attractive option for those uncomfortable about the place of religious education in schools: simply slip the subject into the personal and social education curriculum and the 'problem' of what to do with religious education is solved.

Such an approach is, I believe, dishonest: as was suggested above, the understanding of religion as an end in itself is no more or less important than the study of any other subject. Which other departments would be willing to bypass the centrality of their subject area in favour of the role of accepting responsibility for moral education? The place of religious education in the curriculum is no different, fundamentally, than that of any other subject area. It will contribute and support the hidden curriculum and ethos of the school; it will address directly issues of morality in so far as they relate to the subject matter of religion; it will stand alongside and support programmes of moral and social education.

If accepted, these suggestions do give a specific role for religious education in the development of society, but it is no longer a central, unique or special one. The religious educator will take on board the responsibility of exploring the specific place of religion in the development of society. There can be little doubt that religion, and its rejection, is of vital importance to the nation. Religion is one of the cutting edges through which contemporary society understands itself, but how can religious education appropriate this fact in the classroom? It is to this issue that we must now turn.

The moral ambiguity of religion

Can religion at least contribute to cementing society together? If so, what particular brand of cement can be used? It is imperative, it seems to me, that religious education adopts a hard-nosed and realistic approach to these issues. Given the complexities and tensions of modern society, a starry-eyed, innocent idealism is not likely to do more than paper over the cracks of society. In this respect there are currently two idealistic stances that need to be approached with a healthy scepticism.

Beyond idealism

The first of these idealistic visions has its roots in the belief that the problems of modern society stem from secularization and the loss of religious belief. Society, it suggests, can only genuinely develop if it learns to accept the truth of Christianity, Islam, or whatever form of religion the advocate of this approach adheres to.

The second idealistic approach has its roots in the humanistic belief that the cement of society must be that of the mutual acceptance of our common humanity. Religion, it holds, has throughout history been a source of sectarian tension and violence. If we can learn to hold to our religious beliefs in a more relaxed, less 'fundamentalist' manner, then we might be able to produce a tolerant, humanitarian society.

I do not want to suggest that either of these views, both of which have currency in the contemporary debate regarding religious education, contain no element of truth. However, they have in common an idealism that ignores the complex realities of modern society, and hence will ultimately fail for purely pragmatic reasons.

Say, for example, that religious education was to draw exclusively on the Christian tradition in its attempts to cement society together. Even if Christianity were true, the implementation of such a policy would only add to tensions within society. Adherents of other religions would demand to know, 'Why Christianity?', while secularists and humanists would turn on the rhetorical cries of 'indoctrination'.

Yet if, alternatively, the humanistic programme is implemented, then the cries of the religiously committed of 'secularism' and 'reductionism', and the justified complaints that this approach fails to do justice to the nature of various religious traditions, would be heard. As recent events, such as the Rushdie affair, have demonstrated, a Muslim can no more accept the relative unimportance of his or her faith's teaching in favour of a common humanity than the secular humanist can bypass his or her commitment to a common humanity in favour of an acceptance of the primary value of religious doctrine.

These idealistic approaches both ignore the complexities of contemporary society and proceed by attempting to impose a consensus (on society and on education) in the form of a blueprint that pictures society as they would like it to become. The problem is that there is more than one blueprint. I would like to suggest that there is no simple idealistic solution to the question of the role of religion in the moral development of society, and that if religious education is to have anything to offer this must be made on the basis of a realistic understanding of the nature of religion in society.

Towards a realistic approach

We need to be constantly aware that our pluralistic society as a whole is an ambiguous one. If we do this it quickly becomes clear that any 'consensus' is inevitably going to be a majority one that imposes unacceptable conditions on minority groups. Any programme of education that attempts to impose a 'solution' on the problems of society will inevitably ride roughshod over the reality of the situation. It is by no means clear exactly how religion and morality come together. Is religion, and in which form, ultimately a force for moral progress or a force for the retardation of society? Has society since the Enlightenment progressed or declined? Are we morally better off with or without religion?

There are no simple answers. Take Christianity as an example. An increasing number of Christians, while acknowledging the force for good of their religion, will also now openly accept its dark side: the church's guilt in the areas of anti-semitism, slavery, religious persecution and the like. They also acknowledge that Christianity does not necessarily lead to human fulfilment and the development of better people: it can produce its saints and heroes, but can also produce broken, fearful, guilt-ridden, inadequate individuals.

We need to accept that the history of the relationship of different religious traditions is as likely to be a history of sectarian strife and violence as much as of mutual harmony and tolerance. Look at Northern Ireland/the occupied counties, where Christian fights Christian; look at Sri Lanka where where Hindu fights Buddhist; look at the Punjab where Sikh fights Hindu; look at the Middle East where Christian, Jew and humanist fights Muslim. Indeed it is difficult to pinpoint a contemporary dispute in our world that has descended to the level of violence in which religion is not, to a greater of lesser extent, a prominent factor.

If we take a realistic view of the situation, and have the courage to shrug off idealistic, blinkered, half-baked impressions, then we are faced with the hard fact that, at best, religion does not appear to offer much in the way of a mixture that might bind society together. However, we do not have to end on such a negative note. We may not have found solutions, but there can be no doubt that we have been brought face-to-face with the cutting edge of the relationship between religion and society. If society is to progress and develop then these issues must be addressed openly and honestly. If disparate groups in society are to find ways of living together, then the issues raised here must be approached and dealt with. We may have no solutions, but we do have a very clear agenda that needs to be addressed.

The question for the religious educator thus becomes not so much, 'How can religion contribute to the development of society?' as, 'How can religious education enable its future voters and leaders to approach the religious dimensions of these problems in intelligent and responsible ways?'. We have here a hint of a possible role for religious education: not that of imposing in paternalistic fashion a blueprint of how society should be, but that of enabling pupils to become educated in the nature and tensions of the ambiguity of religion's place in society. In others words, the process of becoming religiously literate is at one and the same time part of the process of education for citizenship. Religious education is at root a moral and social education from the religious perspective.

Religion, citizenship and the classroom

How might religious education approach its primary task of developing literacy in the context of its responsibility for the moral development of individuals and society? I would suggest that it might do so by guiding pupils on their own pilgrimage towards personal integrity, vision and insight in the light of the religious questions of ultimate truth.

Personal integrity

We need to begin by acknowledging and nurturing the integrity the pupils bring with them to the classroom. To fail to do this will lead to a feeling of uprootedness in children. They come to classes with an understanding of the world that parents, friends, community and society have given them, yet this more often that not fails to be acknowledged, respected and valued. For example, a child brought up in an atheistic or agnostic environment, with a basic trust in parents who have told him or her that this is what the world is like, should not have to face a barrage of implicit messages from teachers, rooted in a mistaken desire that the value of religion should be advocated: your tradition is not worth speaking about; you lack sensitivity towards the religious dimension of life; you need to learn to see the world differently; your presuppositions are somehow inadequate.

We have seen this century, in eastern Europe and China, just what can happen to individuals and societies who are not allowed access in an educated way to the traditions and culture of parents and grandparents. Being uprooted from a tradition creates a moral vacuum that can all too easily be exploited by those who believe they have something better to offer. This is experienced most keenly by the Muslim community in Britain, denied as they are at present the same funding that would allow them to bring up their children within the traditions of Islam that the state offers to the Christian and Jewish communities.

By suggesting that the problem of religious understanding lies with children's inadequate vision, rather than in the possibility that they might just be right, is to bypass an agenda that surely should be a central one in our schools. Children are not stupid: they know that many peers, adults and groups in society hold the same attitudes towards religion that they do and they know when they are being patronized.

Such participation leads to tension and even conflict. Religious education teachers are aware of this: they deal with it every day of their working lives. Why bother with a subject that denies the value of your traditions? If your concerns and viewpoint cannot be placed on the agenda, then you opt out of the educational process. Your enthusiasm, energy and insight, that should be at the heart of a flourishing and invigorating investigation of the question of the true nature of the universe, is channelled into discovering various 'deviant', though often very imaginative, ways of making the time spent in 'RE' pass a little quicker, or at least in a more entertaining way!

The moral education of children should be 'child-centred' in so far as it starts with children who indwell a tradition and community. We need then to start with what sociologists describe as the 'primary socialization' of the child. In the early stages of life they learn about themselves and our world by the way in which their environment and those people with primary responsibility for their upbringing react to them. They learn appropriate actions, a language, emotions, values, a belief system in terms of their home life. The meaning of their life, their sense of self-worth and value is linked up with an acceptance of the authority and world view of those who bring them up.

As the child gets older, he or she encounters a series of 'secondary socializations'. The freedom to build up relationships with peers and adults outside of the home environment, exposure to the media, of elements of youth culture, to a broad range of attitudes, beliefs and opinions different from that offered by the security and authority of the home, force children at an early age to begin to come to terms with and discover their place and identity within a complex pluralistic society. By the time the child reaches secondary school, the capacity to live within this wealth of complexity has become highly developed. Pupils come to religious education classes with an extremely sophisticated awareness of their identities within a complex universe. True, for many this awareness may be rooted in a sense of uncertainty and confusion, but the fact that they are aware of this is a testament to the abilities they have already developed.

It is vital to recognize that *all* pupils come to religious education lessons with a religious belief system. It may be highly developed and significant in their lives; it may be a hotchpotch of confused and contradictory ideas; it may be a belief in the reality of some form of religious belief or may be a belief in the falsity or meaningless irrelevance of religion, but it will, inevitably, be there.

If religious education is to start from the child's perspective, then it becomes imperative that classroom activities give children the time and space to begin to reflect on, interpret and understand the nature of the belief system with which they are already operating.

Personal vision and insight

Religious education for citizenship must start from where the pupils are, but it does not stop there. The next stage involves the process of pupils' contextualizing their traditions, of understanding them in relation to other possibilities.

In approaching a variety of belief systems, both religious and non-religious, in an informed manner the pupils will have their understanding of the nature of the universe, of our pluralistic society and of themselves broadened. They will be able to look at the issues from a perspective that frees them from a blinkered attitude, one that accepts unquestioningly what is familiar and rejects without serious thought all that is unfamiliar. As discontented philosophers they will be freed from the limitations of their own world views, freed to develop a vision of new possibilities and options.

By appreciating the values and truth claims of a variety of traditions, they will then be in a position to develop their own self-understanding, to go back to their presuppositions and traditions and to reinterpret and rearticulate them in the light of their developing awareness of other possibilities and claims. This does not mean abandoning their perspectives in the light of others. The phenomenon of 'conversion' from one belief system to another, in the context of formal schooling, is a relatively rare one. It does mean the ability to critically appropriate their tradition in a more intelligent and informed way, to develop their self-understanding, values and beliefs in the light of a broader vision of humanity's complex religious quest.

All of this is not an additional task for the religious education teacher, but part and parcel of the process of becoming religiously literate. If individuals are to develop as responsible citizens we must not give them fish, but teach them how to fish. We must allow them, by both nurturing and challenging their beliefs, to take personal responsibility for their own growth, their value systems and their place as citizens in our society; to accept such responsibility in the light of an intelligent understanding of the relationship of religious questions, truth claims and ambiguity to their ongoing pilgrimage through life. Such citizens will be able to approach their duties as citizens in a democracy with wisdom and insight, above all able to play their part in the task of the next generation of leading a complex pluralistic society towards moral and spiritual growth.

The cement of society, insofar as it contains a religious element in its mixture, lies not in a renewed confessionalism, nor in a resurgent liberalism, but in the development of religiously literate individuals, secure in their own faith, open with integrity to the claims of others, and able to place the human adventure in the context of the ultimate questions with which our universe challenges us.

CHAPTER 7

The Heart of Religious Education

Self-examination

We arrive at the final chapter, with the task ahead of us of drawing together some of the threads of the arguments that have been presented. Starting with the question as to why religious education continues to have an ambiguous position in the curriculum of many schools, we reviewed liberal and confessional models of the subject in the context of the framework and possibilities offered by the 1988 Education Reform Act. At the core of the discussion lay the suggestion that there is a need to move towards a new agenda for religious education, one more relevant to the needs of a diverse, pluralistic western democracy in the 1990s. Such an agenda, it was suggested, should proceed by taking seriously the apparently paradoxical themes of religious truth and religious ambiguity, themes that could be held together by adopting a model of education as pilgrimage. Finally, we look at ways in which such a pilgrimage might help produce a developing maturity both in individuals and in society.

The key thread linking together the diverse arguments we have looked at is the suggestion that contemporary religious education needs to take a long hard look at itself, discard much of the surplus baggage it has picked up over the years and in the process rediscover its heart and its soul. Put another way, it needs to discover a sense of its own integrity.

But what exactly constitutes integrity? Standard dictionary definitions refer us to the notions of wholeness, soundness, honesty and uprightness. Perhaps the core of integrity lies in the notion of the 'bottom line': thrown into the complexity and challenges of modern life, the person with integrity is the one who, in a spirit of integrated self-understanding, with a coherent insight into the value and worth of themselves, and with an openness and truthfulness towards those around them, has the courage of their convictions when all of this is challenged. One who, when faced with the 'bottom line', is not in danger of trespassing over it: one able to say, 'Here I stand, I can do no other'.

Has religious education any integrity, any bottom line, any soul? One way to answer this question is to imagine what a school might look like if religious education were taken off the curriculum. What difference would this make to the life of that learning community? What happens if we peel off the layers of its work and activity? Do we discover any bottom line that only religious education can provide, so that the school is lacking something of real significance if religious education is not there? Or will its activities simply be taken up and incorporated into other curriculum areas, so that its absence is hardly noticed?

Is religious education a 'subject for all seasons', skilfully adapting itself to fit into whatever the school, politicians, educationalists or society requires of it at any given time, in an effort to gain acceptance? Or has it a vision and integrity, a coherence, openness and self-assurance that enables it to contribute something positive and unique to the life of the educational community?

The integrity of religion

How might religious education approach its subject matter, the phenomenon of religion itself, with integrity? We have suggested that integrity here is not to be found in programmes that seek to utilize religion for political or social ends, as an ingredient in the cement of social engineering. Still less is it to be found in programmes that pre-package religion into something safe, bland and unchallenging. Rather, the integrity of religion is to be found at its heart, in the ultimate questions about ourselves, society, the environment and the universe itself that it poses, and above all in the twin issues of religious truth and religious ambiguity.

Ultimate questions

Religion at its heart asks questions, not the minor questions tied down to local concerns and needs, but the major ones, the ultimate questions that challenge us to ask after ultimate truth and meaning.

Questions about our humanity. Our humanity has produced its Hitlers and its Mother Teresas, its symphonies and gas chambers. As human beings are we more than a mixture of simple atoms and molecules; are we more than adequately functioning biological animals? Is the human spirit more than just a bundle of emotions and animal instincts? Is its creativity no more than a futile cry, a cry lost in the emptiness of a decaying universe? Has life any ultimate meaning and purpose, or are we doomed to either survive pragmatically or else embrace nihilism and despair? Were we created in the image of God, or do we owe our existence to the brute fact that our universe is simply there?

Questions about society. How and why do we relate to our fellow men and women? What standards, values, morality and virtues should we adopt? Is it simply a case of survival of the fittest? Of personal achievement rewarded and failure punished? What responsibility do we have towards the weak, the helpless, the 'deviant'? Perhaps, most fundamentally of all, on what grounds do we answer such questions? How does our understanding of the nature of reality, of its source and origin, shape the answers we give?

Questions about our environment. The green agenda is now firmly before us, no longer the child of 'cranks' who only eat vegetables and enjoy wearing sandals. It is an agenda now nurtured, in appearance at least, by governments of the western democracies. Pollution, global warming, endangered species, the misuse of scarce resources: all are no longer side issues. The future of our children, our children's children, and indeed of life on earth is dependent on how we respond to these challenges. The challenge to humanity seems clear, yet the cynical might point out the futility of all our efforts. Does not the second law of thermodynamics teach us that the order of the cosmos is constantly breaking apart, heading inevitably towards the 'heat death' that will bring ultimate chaos and disorder? Is humanity merely living on borrowed time, and will not all its environmental efforts prove ultimately futile as nature leads eventually towards an environment no longer capable of sustaining life on our planet? Yet does not the ancient myth tell us that God created the universe, and saw that it was good?

Questions about the universe. Questions about cosmology, origins and quantum physics. The ontological questions of the medieval theologians and philosophers are still with us, albeit in different forms. Why is it that there is something rather than nothing? Do we need to invoke a creator God, or can we settle for the notion of a self-creating universe? Accident or design? Ultimate order or ultimate chaos? Questions that have no simple answers, yet about which three things seem clear. First, the disciplines of theological and natural science are once again speaking with each other after centuries of mutual distrust and even antagonism, and their debates form one of the key cutting edges in the ongoing expansion of human understanding of our universe. Second, the answers we choose to give fundamentally alter the way in which we approach our earlier questions about the environment, society and humanity. Third, we cannot avoid giving at least a contingent answer to these questions, since to put them on one side as irrelevant or simply unanswerable is to actually give an answer of sorts and so turns our attention back once again to the former questions.

Truth

Religion does not just ask these ultimate questions, it also provides answers, makes claims about what is ultimately true, ultimately of value. The religious world views, of Islam and Buddhism, of Judaism and Sikhism and of countless others, offer humanity the truth, not only about our moral codes and self-understanding, but the truth about our world, our universe, about reality itself. Yet we must speak of 'truths' rather than 'truth'. We are faced with a plurality of truths that can be held together in harmony only with great difficulty, and at the enormous cost of ignoring the fact that for the vast majority of believers *their* truth is the only one, and *their* truth thus stands in opposition to the truth of others.

Alternatively, of course, many choose to reject religious truth in its entirety, preferring to start not from a transcendent reality but from an immanent one. Here there are no gods or powers above and beyond space and time, no notions of a transcendent being. They offer us truth on the premise that religion is fundamentally illusionary, false and misguided. Here again, the truths of such secular systems vary and contradict one another: humanism, liberalism, existentialism, pragmatism, nihilism, positivism, Marxism, capitalism.

Truth matters if human life is to progress in harmony with reality. Few would choose the option of openly living a lie rather than pursuing truth. The plurality of ultimate truth claims should not mesmerize us into thinking that this pursuit of truth is futile. We have learnt in this century that there is no clear distinction between knowledge and belief. We have come to accept that all human knowledge is contingent and provisional. Even those religious groups who hold fast to a belief in a clear and unambiguous revelation will, in the main, accept the human need for a deeper insight and understanding of such knowledge.

Truth is reached through an ongoing process of understanding and misunderstanding, of trial and error, of shifts from one paradigm to another. We make the best of the evidence that we have available, and test the results in the light of our later experience, seeking deeper coherence and meaning, and being willing to reject that which, like astrology and Newtonian science, we learn to see as fundamentally flawed. This is, at root, what education is all about. At root education demands that contented pigs learn to become discontented philosophers. Ultimately education must be a process of learning to become fully human; the core of its being must be humanistic.

Ambiguity

If we put ultimate questions and ultimate truth together we arrive inevitably at ambiguity. It is a simple fact that the questions and answers do not match up, or at least not all of them. This should not surprise us, since we are human, not divine: we cannot simply adopt a God-like perspective on ourselves and our universe; we cannot float above it and imagine ourselves divine. It is part of the nature of our humanity that we do not know all the answers. We look with amazement at the arrogance of those philosophers, above all at the example of logical positivism, that offered us ultimate truth and final solutions. We reconstruct our past only with hesitancy, we all struggle daily to make sense of the present, and when we look into the future we can do little more than speculate. Ambiguity is simply part and parcel of what it means to be human.

What is surprising, though, is the way we in the west have struggled against this basic feature of our reality, the way we have demanded clarity and certainty and have acted as if we could be gods. Perhaps this reflects an inbuilt insecurity on our part, a desire to control, dominate and utilize for our own ends. Some would claim this is a specifically modern western attitude towards the world. We seem to have in the west a tendency to prefer knowledge and control to wisdom and insight.

We need to learn to embrace ambiguity, to rediscover a sense of the exhilaration of adventure and exploration. We need to be willing once more to risk sailing off the edge of the world, to (if you'll forgive me this one) 'seek new life and new civilisations and boldly go where no one has gone before'! We need to accept the challenge and the risk of being truly human.

It is here, in the combination of ultimate questions, ultimate truth and of ambiguity, that the integrity of religious education is to be found, here where it discovers its 'bottom line', where its heart and soul lies. It is in this pilgrimage that religious education can offer something to the process of learning that other subjects could not replace.

The integrity of the teacher

The old *confessional* model of religious education viewed commitment to the Christian faith as a fundamental prerequisite for anyone undertaking the task of teaching religious education. If the aim is to nurture and educate in the Christian faith, than the absence of such faith on the part of the teacher makes the task an impossible one.

Reacting against this, and acutely aware of the accusation of 'indoctrination', the old *liberal* model demanded on the part of the teacher not commitment but openness, indeed, not just any form of openness, but a rigorous and carefully guarded neutrality. To ask the question as to the truth of a religious doctrine was simply not on the agenda.

Both approaches offer contrasting and conflicting pictures of the professionalism and integrity expected of a teacher of religious education. Both, though, had in common the belief that the teacher should, and could, play the role of arbiter between religious disputes. There is buried here a notion of the teacher as 'expert', one with the answers to the complex questions religion gives birth to. It is a notion linked, I feel, with the erroneous belief that to teach something is to advocate it. If indeed the teacher is the 'expert' in *this* sense, the advocate of the truth about religion, then there need be little wonder that the issue of the professionalism of the teacher revolved around the tension between commitment and neutrality. It is on the ability of teachers to play the right game in terms of this tension between neutrality and commitment that their integrity was to be judged.

The question of neutrality versus commitment seems to me to be fundamentally irrelevant. Given that every teacher of religious education will inevitably go into the classroom with a particular commitment, a particular set of attitudes and beliefs, the expectation that these beliefs are suspended and put on one side seems to me to be fundamentally dishonest, requiring the teacher, ultimately, to portray a false picture of themselves to their pupils. Not only is it dishonest, in the long term it actually fails to work: in reality the suspension on one's presuppositions cannot be hidden. Pupils should not be underestimated here: they are skilled at seeing through such a farce and quick to pick up, through nuances of expression and by reading between the lines, a fairly good approximation of where exactly in the spectrum of religious belief their teacher is coming from.

The dangers of such presuppositions on the part of the teacher, the reality that they might deliberately or inadvertently allow their teaching to be swayed by their beliefs, are far less if such beliefs are on the public agenda, that pupils are made aware explicitly just where their teacher actually stands. By identifying explicitly such information, pupils have a much better chance of perceiving any attempt to misuse it. I would thus suggest openness and honesty on the part of the teacher regarding their own religious beliefs in the classroom as the first step towards their own professional integrity.

Of course this is only a first step. The heart of teachers' professional integrity should be rooted in their ability either to place their role as educator before that of their concern with their own belief systems, or else to understand that their belief systems actually demand they act as professional educators. As educators their task is to help produce religious literacy in their pupils, to enable them to mature in their ability to think and communicate about religious issues. For some this will be a genuine challenge, one on which their claims to integrity will ultimately be decided. For others, the relationship between their faith and their professional role as educators will be an unproblematical one, particularly if their faith itself is committed to openness, freedom and an avoidance of hypocrisy.

If, as educators, we take seriously the complexity and ambiguity of religion, then a key task in our developing integrity as teachers will be that of enabling students to stop thinking of ourselves as experts who can offer the right answers to, or give the 'official school line' about, religion. As our pupils become increasingly literate about religion, they must at the same time learn to realize that their teacher can be no more than a fellow pilgrim and learner. They must be helped to accept that, while they can turn to their teacher for advice and guidance, support and encouragement on their journey, they cannot also expect solutions and answers.

The response to the question, 'But is it true?' or, 'But what do *you* think?', needs to be along the lines of, 'Why are you asking me? If I knew the answers I wouldn't be here teaching you would I?'. Or alternatively, 'Well, as a Christian, I think this. Of course other Christians might say something different, and Muslims of course would certainly not agree with me. By the way, what do you think? And why are you so interested in my beliefs? Do you really think I know the answers?'.

The integrity of the teacher lies then not in their ability to hide or admit their own beliefs, but in their ability to put such questions on one side as being, though always present, ultimately irrelevant to the educational process. Integrity lies rather in the ability to forego the role of expert and advocate and concentrate instead on the task of enabling one's students' own education in religion to develop.

The theologian and philosopher Kierkegaard understood this situation better than most. He was happy to write books under assumed names, offering arguments which, whilst he had grappled with them at some time in his life, nevertheless he actually did not agree with. If you read Kierkegaard aware of this fact then immediately you are forced to think for yourself; you cannot settle back and assume that what you are being told is actually what Kierkegaard intends you to come away with. You are faced with the task not of sitting at the feet of a master, but listening to a teacher who demands that you think for yourself, and has no desire that you simply agree with what is said.

It is important to realize that such an approach to teaching through 'indirect communication' or playing 'devil's advocate' has nothing to do with dishonesty. The teacher will need to be sure that pupils are aware of the game they are playing, and approach such lessons, in which the teacher is essentially 'role playing', with more than a touch of irony. An excellent example of such a teaching strategy in operation, for those a little daunted by the prospect of reading Kierkegaard himself, is to be found in Peter Vardy's book *God of Our Fathers?* (1987). Essentially a primer in the philosophy of religion, and an increasingly popular A-level text, it offers the reader a number of different ways of understanding the concept 'God', but without advocating any of them, The clue to Vardy's own position is to be found in hints in the text, and above all in the title of the book itself, but by the time you work that out it is irrelevant, since you have already been drawn into considering the various options for yourself.

The professional integrity of the teacher lies, then, in the ability to make the intelligent appropriation of religious questions and issues the heart of what goes on in the classroom, in the process acknowledging one's beliefs yet denying that they have any value or relevance to the teaching process itself.

Integrity in the school

Given that the subject of religion is approached with the kind of integrity that has been suggested, and that this is paralleled in the professionalism of teachers, what signs of integrity might we look for in terms of the place of religious education itself within the curriculum, of its role in the pastoral life of the school, of its input into the broader community, and above all of the vision it offers the school?

Religious education can operate with integrity in schools only if its status, importance and place in the curriculum are assured by governors and headteachers. The subject can have no real integrity if it relies for its status on the force of personality and hard graft of the subject teacher. In this context it is perhaps worthwhile reminding ourselves of the legal obligations of schools in this respect, together with DfE and NCC advice as to what the law implies.

The law requires that religious education to be taught according to an Agreed Syllabus. The DfE advises that such syllabuses should assume:

> that there will be reasonable time available for the study of religious education, and that religious education has equal standing with core and foundation subjects (NCC, 1992, p.56).

Further, the NCC advises that:

> Where possible pupils should take a religious studies course to GCSE,

and that:

> The quality of religious teaching should match that in other National Curriculum subjects (NCC, 1992, p.57).

Against this background the government has stated quite unambiguously in the context of a White Paper that 'there is a need to give further impetus to the development of religious education in schools' (DfE, 1992, para. 8.5), and it has also underlined the fact that Inspectors must now report specifically on a school's delivery of the spiritual aspects of the curriculum.

Schools, then, are expected to teach to a syllabus that assumes religious education is of equal standing to National Curriculum subjects, and give a reasonable time allocation for this, together with ensuring that teaching is of a similar quality to that of other subjects. Further, unless it can be shown to be impossible, pupils should take a GCSE examination in religious education. A school is open to challenge from the Inspectorate if it fails to achieve this, and it is the government's stated wish that the position of religious education in schools be enhanced.

Students have an entitlement to a broad and balanced curriculum in which religious education is secured in its proper place. Responsibility for seeing that this happens lies not with the beleaguered religious education teacher, but with the headteacher and school governors. Only when this has been achieved can the subject take its place with integrity in schools.

Given its proper status in the life of the school, with the appropriate level of staffing, resources and timetable allocation that this requires, it falls to the religious education teacher to implement the Agreed Syllabus in a manner that reflects the integrity of the subject.

Of course education must be concerned with Britain's Christian heritage; with the moral and social development of children; with their pastoral well-being; with equal opportunities; with building a framework towards an integrated multicultural society. No one in their right mind would suggest otherwise. However, remove religious education from the curriculum and all these themes should still be dealt with clearly and vigorously by the school, since they are important to all curriculum areas. Every subject has the duty of dealing with them in terms of its own content, subject matter and outlook. Peel these themes away and we get to the soul of religious education, its task of placing all these themes in the context of ultimate questions, of the issues of religious truth and ambiguity. And these issues need to be pursued with the same academic vigour, the same search for wisdom and insight, the same concern for the development of skills and literacy as any other subject on the curriculum.

Religious education has a primary duty to enhance a school's curriculum by ensuring that the study of religious issues and questions flourishes. Once this is in order it can contribute to the wider life of the school: by enhancing and enriching cross-curricular issues and themes; by playing its distinctive role in the pastoral provision of the school; by contributing to the development of the local community.

This contribution would seem to me to be rooted in two areas. First, by nurturing and enhancing the religious and areligious world views of pupils and the wider school community, in a spirit of tolerance, openness and honesty. Second, by being willing to challenge the school, to make available to it the reality of the ultimate questions it is concerned with; to offer the school a vision of education as pilgrimage towards that which is ultimately true; to question it when its focus becomes narrow and blinkered; to gently ease the community as a whole into seeing itself as a community of discontented philosophers, thirsty for truth in the midst of the complexity, ambiguities and possibilities of our complex society.

Why teach religious education?

'So you're a teacher then: what is it exactly you teach?' We have come full circle and find ourselves back at our starting point. Perhaps, in retrospect, my stock answer, 'Children' was indeed a little dishonest, possibly the response was itself lacking in integrity. Might I not have been guilty of leaving my questioners content in their prejudices and misapprehensions, of taking the easy way out and avoiding the challenge offered?

Could I not have answered:

> Religious education: because we are given but one short life and the way we live it matters; because the ultimate questions matter; because religious and areligious truth matters; because the reality of ambiguity matters; because it matters if we are contented pigs or discontented philosophers; because it matters whether or not we are religiously literate; because the integrity of religious education raises issues that lie at the heart of what it means to be human, at the heart of society, at the heart of our environment, and at the heart of that which is ultimately true about reality.

But that, or course, is only my answer and the chances are that I am wrong. *Professional* religious education teachers must answer for themselves, since to learn to fish is of far greater value than being given a fish. If this book has served to stimulate your thinking a little further then it has achieved its task.

References

Church Times (1992). Letter from Rev'd John Greenway, 2 October.

Department for Education (1992) *Choice and Diversity: A New Framework for Schools,* London: HMSO.

Department of Education and Science (1988) *Education Reform Act 1988*, London HMSO.

Dewey, J. (1966) *Democracy and Education*, London: The Free Press.

Elliot, T. S. (1974) 'Burnt Norton', in *Collected Poems 1909-1962,* London: Faber & Faber.

Fageant, J. and Mercier, S. C. (1988) *Skills in Religious Education. Book One*, London: Hienemann.

Gay, P. (1977) *The Enlightenment: An Interpretation. The Science of Freedom*, London: Norton.

Grimmitt, M. (1987) *Religious Education and Human Development*, Essex: McCrimmon.

McCreery, E. (1993) *Worship in the Primary School*, London: David Fulton.

National Curriculum Council (1992) *Starting out with the National Curriculum: An Introduction to the National Curriculum and Religious Education* (DES Circular, 3/89), York: NCC.

Simon, U. (1978) *A Theology of Auschwitz*, London: SCM.

Sutherland, S. R. (1984) *Faith and Ambiguity*, London: SCM.

Vardy, P. (1987) *God of Our Fathers?*, London: Darton, Longman and Todd.

Further Reading

Cox, E. and Cairns, J. (1989) *Reforming Religious Education*, London: Kogan Page.

Cuppitt, D. (1972) *Crisis of Moral Authority*, London: SCM.

Francis, L. and Thatcher, A. (eds) (1990) *Christian Perspectives for Education*, Leominster: Fowler Wright.

Hulmes, E. (1979) *Commitment and Neutrality in Religious Education*, London: Chapman.

Lochhead, D. (1988) *The Dialogical Imperative*, London: SCM.

Newbigin, L. (1986) *Foolishness to the Greeks*, London: SPCK.

Tracy, D. (1987) *Plurality and Ambiguity*, London: SCM.

Watson, B. (ed.) (1992) *Priorities in Religious Education*, London: Falmer Press.

Index